D1526236

About the Book

Here is the gripping story of a madman who almost conquered the world in our time. Adolf Hitler: World War I corporal, gangster chief, dictator, generalissimo. In this dramatic account author John Devaney traces the career of a disturbed personality who made a precarious living in the Vienna underworld and finally became deranged on the center stage of history.

Hitler's life bears resemblance to the lives of some gangsters. But while mobsters have killed scores, Hitler destroyed millions of lives and enslaved millions more—all because of his psychic need to be number one. His life is a sordid tale of double cross and brutish violence—and Devaney makes no attempt to gloss it over. Here we see the wonder of how the man duped nearly 60,000,000 Germans and became their revered leader.

But that was only the beginning for this sick dictator and his henchmen. He ordered the destruction of millions of Jews and other peoples. He terrified the rulers of Europe. In a secret memo he plotted the enslavement and killing of millions of Americans. His Nazi swastika fluttered from near the Arctic Circle to the Sahara, from the beaches of the Atlantic to the gateway cities of the Orient.

This vivid account carries Hitler through his time of success to his self-destruction in a Berlin bunker.

HITLER

Mad Dictator of World War II

by John Devaney

G. P. PUTNAM'S SONS, NEW YORK

Library of Congress Cataloging in Publication Data
Devaney, John.
    Hitler, mad dictator of World War II.
    Includes index.
    SUMMARY: Traces the life of Adolf Hitler from his
youth to his self-destruction in a Berlin bunker.
    1. Hitler, Adolf, 1889-1945—Juvenile literature. 2.
Heads of state—Germany—Biography—Juvenile literature.
3. Germany—Politics and government—1933-1945—Juvenile literature. [1. Hitler, Adolf—1889-1945. 2. Heads of
state. 3. Germany—Politics and government—1933-1945]
I. Title.
DD247.H5D4775 1978 943.086′092′4 [B] [92]
77-21057
ISBN 0-399-20627-2

For Barbara,
who understands why

Contents

Acknowledgments

No one can count how many millions of words have been written about Adolf Hitler. I have tried to read as many of those words as I could, and I am indebted to these authors and their books for much of the material in these pages. John Toland, in his recent two-volume biography *Adolf Hitler,* unearthed many unknown facts. A former World War II German soldier, Joachim C. Fest, has done an incisive analysis of what he called this "unperson" in his *Hitler.* Perhaps the basic book for anyone who wants to understand Hitler and the Germany of his time is William L. Shirer's masterful *The Rise and Fall of the Third Reich.* And for a look at what it was like to be one of Hitler's accomplices, I recommend Albert Speer's *Inside the Third Reich.* Other helpful works were Louis Snyder's *Hitler and Nazism, The Ultra Secret* by F. W. Winterbotham, *The Mind of Adolf Hitler* by Walter C. Langer, and *Hitler,* edited by George H. Stein.

—J. D.

1

"No Bullet with Your Name on It!"

The German soldiers cowered on the mucky ground. Bullets whined above their spiked helmets. Then, suddenly, the loud and angry clatter of the machine guns ceased.

The soldiers cautiously raised their heads and peered up the darkening slope. Somewhere at the top of this hill, masked by the smoke of exploding shells and the murky evening dusk, squatted a French machine-gun nest that was spraying them with streams of death.

One of the German soldiers hugging the hill was a corporal. His face was thin and waxy white. Sharp cheekbones jutted out over a drooping mustache. His blue eyes glared upward into the gloom. An expression of rage contorted his face. This was the face, the eyes of Adolf Hitler, corporal in the Imperial German Army of Kaiser Wilhelm II.

Hitler glanced to his left and right. The hill around his patrol was being rocked by shells lobbed from French and British positions on the other side of the hill near Ypres in France. He knew that he and his patrol could not hug this open ground much longer.

Hitler and the seven other Germans rose slowly on hands and knees. They crawled along the side of the hill, using any bump of ground as a shield between themselves and where they thought that machine-gun nest was on the top of the hill.

Suddenly Hitler slammed his chest and face into the wet ground. He had seen two telltale tongues of fire leap out of the murk no more than fifty feet away; then he heard the awful roar of the machine guns.

Heavy slugs bit into the mud around the patrol. The hunks of metal stitched holes across chests and backs and tore open legs, severing them almost in half. Men screamed. Their bodies were thrown around the hill by the whizzing trains of bullets.

Not one bullet touched Hitler. He gripped the earth, motionless. Then the *rat-tat-tat* clatter began to dwindle amid the shrieks of men dying.

The shrieks became moans, men calling for help or for their mothers. Then the moans became whimpers, and after a minute, even they ceased. A hush settled over the scene, and soon the only sounds were from far away—what one American general in this World War I later called "the strange mournful mutter of the battlefield."

Hitler slowly raised his head. One grimy hand held his spiked helmet; the other gripped his rifle. Around him four men lay dead, blood leaking from their torn bodies.

Hitler waved a clenched hand at the three others of the patrol who were still alive. He indicated he knew where the machine guns were. Quickly, on hands and knees, they scurried, crablike, around the side of the hill.

Moments later Hitler and his patrol popped up onto a hillock directly above the French machine gunners.

"Surrender!" the Germans shouted. The surprised French spun to look into the black barrels of German rifles.

12

Hitler and his three comrades led the captured French soldiers across the shell-pocked no-man's-land and into the German trenches. The next day an officer recommended that the four be decorated. A few days later Hitler and the other three reported to a tent a few hundred meters behind the front-line trenches, where the medals were being handed out.

When Hitler arrived at the tent, he saw that it was jammed with soldiers. A captain instructed Hitler and the three other soldiers from the List Regiment to come back in an hour to receive their medals.

Hitler and the others walked away from the tent. Minutes later a French 88 shell whined down out of the sky and crashed into the tent. The shell's spray of iron killed everyone within the tent and some twenty meters around it.

A stunned Hitler walked back to the leaky-roofed, rat-infested dugout behind the front lines where he was quartered. It was not the first time he had walked away from a place where a shell was about to make a deadly hit.

One afternoon a few months earlier he had been eating out of his mess kit with several other soldiers, crouched against the wall of a trench. Suddenly Hitler stared up at the sky. "A voice seemed to be saying to me," he wrote years later, " 'Get up and go over there.' "

Hitler looked around but saw no one. Looking back at the soldiers around him he realized they had not heard a voice. Again, he said, the voice repeated insistently, "Get up and go over there."

Hitler stood, picked up his mess kit, and walked a few hundred meters down the trench. He sat down. A minute later there was a blinding flash of an explosion. Hitler was hurled back against the rear wall of the trench.

Eyes blinking, he staggered to his feet, gripping the wall for support. He looked down the trench to where he had been eating. All his companions were strewn about like rag dolls, torn apart by a shell that had landed exactly where he and they had been sitting.

The List Regiment soldiers talked with awe of Hitler's seeming invulnerability. They told each other, only half-jokingly, that there was an invisible ring around Hitler that deflected bullets. One soldier, Private Hans Mend, said to him, *"Mensch, für dich gibt es keine Kugel"*—"Man, they don't have a bullet with your name on it."

The other soldiers of the List Regiment thought Hitler led both a charmed life and a strange one. Seldom did they see a smile on his putty-complexioned face. "If he ever laughs," a List soldier told another, "it's only when he goes by himself down to a cellar."

His uniform hung loosely on his dumpy five-foot-nine, 150-pound frame. His short mustache drooped. There was, a soldier said, usually "a lively glow" in his blue eyes. Often he sat in a corner of the smelly dugout, sketching scenes that he had seen at the front. "He is just an odd character," another soldier said, "and lives in his own world, but otherwise, he's a nice fellow."

When the List Regiment filed out of the trenches to march to a village behind the lines for a few days of rest, most of the soldiers rushed to taverns to eat, drink, sing, and carouse with women. Hitler squatted alone in the barracks, polishing his rifle and sharpening his bayonet. Helmet tipped to the side of his head, clutching the knifelike bayonet, he looked like one of the old Indian fighters he'd read about in Wild West stories of the American plains. Those stories had been his favorite books as a boy.

"The Austrian never relaxes," another soldier said one morning, watching Hitler reassemble his cleaned rifle. "He always acts as if we'd lose the war if he weren't on the job every minute."

Some of the soldiers were puzzled by Hitler's soldierly ardor. After all, he hadn't been born a German: He was an Austrian. Many Germans looked down on Austrians as being happy-go-lucky and soft, lacking the inner iron of true Germans.

Hitler yearned to be thought of as a true German. He had been born only a few miles from the German border, spoke German with a South German's accent, and considered himself 100 percent German. All the Germans who had been born in Austria and other areas around Germany, he often argued, were Germans. Germany should swallow up those areas and make them part of the German Reich, which means empire. Riding on a troop train to the battle-fields of France in the fall of 1914, after the First World War had begun, he had seen the sun rise blood-red over the sparkling Rhine River. It was his first view of this river—a shrine to all Germans. The soldiers on the train began to sing "The Watch on the Rhine," a patriotic song, and Hitler, listening to the words, said later that he had felt "as if my heart would burst from my chest."

In battle Hitler seemed eager to prove he was as brave as any German. Once he and his commanding officer were trapped between two hoses of fires from enemy machine guns. Hitler pushed his commander into a ditch, drew the fire toward himself, then ducked to safety. For a number of acts of heroism he had been awarded the Iron Cross Second Class. Later the Iron Cross First Class, the highest award any German enlisted man could receive, was pinned to his gray tunic.

He had been at the front for two years, from 1914 to 1916, without being even scratched, while comrades dropped all around him. In one 1914 battle the List Regiment's 3,500 troops had marched out of a swirling early-morning fog and charged toward a line of British troops. After three days of fighting only 1,700 List soldiers still stood, and many of them were swathed in bloody bandages. Hitler had seen men cut down on his left and right, and a bullet had torn through his sleeve; but he hadn't been hit.

By the spring of 1916 only a handful of those 1,700 soldiers were still with the regiment, and of those, many had been wounded in battles where 20,000 men died in a single day.

Late in June, 1916, the List Regiment moved into the trenches along the Somme River to block a British-French assault. The battle soon became known as the Battle of the Somme. More than 1,000,000 men were killed on both sides. After two months of that bloody slaughter, with men charging across the barbed wire of no-man's-land to be blown away amid the roar and smoke of bursting shells, the armies had moved only a few hundred yards.

Late in that battle a shell exploded in a trench near the spot where Hitler was balled up in sleep. A hunk of iron fragment smashed into his thigh. Writhing with pain as the blood gushed down the side of his leg, Hitler tried to push away stretcher-bearers who wanted to carry him to a first-aid station. His hypnotic eyes were fixed on his commander, Lieutenant Fritz Wiedemann. He gasped, "It isn't so bad, Lieutenant, right? I can still stay with you, I mean, stay with the regiment! Can't I?"

He was sent to a hospital in Germany, where he recovered—no killer bullet still had come to him with his name on it. "From the mud of the Somme to the white beds of this wonderful place!" he exulted. But once he could walk, he insisted on being returned to the muddy shell-blasted trenches of France.

Other soldiers began to suspect that this strange Austrian had no home anywhere else. Rarely did he receive a letter or a package of food. When others offered to share their packages with him, he angrily refused. "The poor devil," said Private Mend, "is going through plenty and doesn't even know for whom in Germany he is risking his life. . . . The trenches are his world."

Back among his comrades of the List Regiment, Hitler usually sat in a corner, his nose poked into a book or his head hanging over a sketch pad as he drew scenes of French villages. But when the other soldiers talked about politics, he leaped to his feet and immediately began to shout his opinions.

"Communist Marxists and Jews in Germany are stabbing the German soldier in the back," he growled, eyes flashing, while the other soldiers stared. He had seen them himself, he said, standing on soapboxes on street corners in Berlin and saying that the Allied blockade was starving Germany to death. "They are lies compounded by liars who want us to surrender," Hitler shouted in his hollow-sounding voice, which could make a table vibrate. "The Jews and Communist Marxists are seeking to destroy the fatherland."

Another soldier began to argue that the German army would be overwhelmed by the British and French, freshened by their new American Allies, and that the Allied sea blockade was starving Germany of food and ammunition.

"Never!" retorted Hitler. "A German victory is as certain as the amen at the end of a prayer!"

"That Hitler," a soldier said of him, "he would keep on fighting until every German woman was wearing her husband's medals and every husband was dead."

But by the fall of 1918 the German army was reeling backward toward Germany, exhausted, bled white, short of food and ammunition. On the night of October 13 the List Regiment fell into trenches on a hill south of Werwick, Belgium. As dusk began to descend over the German trenches, British guns opened up with a barrage that flashed streaks of stabbing light around the Germans. The earth shook from the pounding of shells.

Hitler burrowed into a shallow trench on the hill. Suddenly, near midnight, he heard the cry of "Gas!" The British were dropping shells of mustard gas, the wind blowing the sweet-smelling, lung-scorching poison gas into the faces of the pinned-down Germans.

Hitler slapped on his gas mask. So did others around him. But

17

some soldiers, thinking the tight mask was suffocating them, ripped it off. They died almost instantly as the gas seared their throats and lungs. "It caught him by the throat," was the way one soldier described how a companion died, "and flung him back choking, gurgling, suffocating, dying."

By dawn the ground was littered with dead Germans. Hitler, his gas mask still on, rose. The shelling seemed to have lifted. It hadn't. With a staccato *crump! crump!* a row of gas bombs hit along the side of the hill. The soldiers were enveloped in clouds of gas that seeped through the masks. Men fell to the ground, grasping their throats and eyes, screaming, dying within a few minutes.

Hitler threw off his mask and rubbed his burning eyes. He hurried down the side of the hill to get away from the gas. Around him he could see only murky figures. Tears streamed down his swollen red face.

At the bottom of the hill he thought he might faint from the intensity of the pain in his eyes. He was told to take a message back to headquarters.

"I stumbled and tottered back with burning eyes," he later wrote, "taking with me my last report of the war. A few hours later my eyes had turned into glowing coals and everything had grown dark around me."

A few days later, still blind, Corporal Adolf Hitler lay on the floor of a hospital train that was carrying him and hundreds of other blind, maimed, and crippled German soldiers back to Germany and life in a defeated and occupied country.

Once, while arguing with other soldiers, he had muttered "You will hear much about me. Just wait until my time comes."

His time indeed would come. Within fifteen years after he was blinded on that hill, he stood astride Germany as the dictator of 60,000,000 people. And all around the globe people listened with awe and fear as he called for destruction and annihilation. He became the warlord of a terrifying, blitzkrieging army, led by screaming Stuka dive-bombers and armored vehicles spitting death. He conquered more territory than any generalissimo in modern history. His Nazi swastika fluttered from near the Arctic Circle to the hot sands of the Sahara, from the beaches of the Atlantic to the gateway cities of the Orient. His U-boats prowled the shores of the United States, sinking ships that could see the lights of New York and Philadelphia. In a secret memo he plotted the enslavement and killing of millions of Americans.

Adolf Hitler: World War I corporal. Gangster chief. Dictator. Generalissimo. The story of how close he came to conquering the world began, he later said, as two teenagers walked down a dark street of a small city in Austria.

2

"I Will Be Something!"

The two sixteen-year-old boys strode along the street, boots echoing on the cobblestones. Yellow blobs of light from flickering candles or kerosene lamps showed from only a few windows of the steepled houses as they passed. An occasional horse and carriage click-clacked down the streets, the sounds fading into the midnight darkness.

One of the boys—he was the shorter—was striding so swiftly that his friend, tall and thin, had to jog at his heels to stay even.

The taller boy was August Kubizek, who was called Gustl. He was the son of an upholsterer, and he hoped one day to become a composer or the conductor of a symphony orchestra.

His shorter companion was Adolf Hitler. His face was long and olive-complexioned, split by a thin nose and topped by a forehead that sloped at a sharp angle to his high brown hair. The hair was combed backward in flowing waves. He was wearing the fashionable clothes worn by the dandies of Austria in this year 1905: frilled shirt; wide, flowing neckpiece; swallow-tailed jacket; tight pants. A thin mustache made him look older than sixteen.

As he walked, Hitler had the rapt expression of someone listening to faraway music. He and Gustl had just left the opera house there in Linz, a city perched on the bank of the Danube River. The two friends had watched a performance of *Rienzi,* an opera by Richard Wagner, Hitler's favorite composer. Hitler was fascinated by the fairy-tale story of Rienzi, a poor boy of ancient Rome who becomes the ruler of a vast empire and then is murdered by assassins.

Usually, after a performance of *Rienzi* or any opera, Hitler gushed for hours about the performance. Gustl usually listened. When Adolf spoke, Gustl once said, "It seemed like a volcano erupting, as though something were bursting out of him. All he wanted from me was one thing—silent agreement."

But now it was Adolf who was silent. When Gustl tried to speak, Adolf hushed him. The two walked out of Linz, the last buildings receding in the darkness behind them. They began to ascend a steep hill called the Feinberg. Hitler walked faster and faster, "as if propelled by an invisible force," Gustl later recalled.

At the top of the Feinberg Hitler looked down on moonlit Linz, only a few dots of light showing. The winding Danube shimmered in the moonlight.

Hitler turned and grasped the hands of his friend. He began to talk about Rienzi and how he had risen from a poor boyhood to become a great man. That would happen to him, Hitler said. He, too, one day would be great and the ruler of an empire.

On and on Hitler raved, the prophecies of his greatness seeming to soar out of his mouth and lift him up. Gustl stared, fascinated. Gustl had listened as Hitler raved on about many of his dreams—how he would become a famous painter or an architect, the builder of great monuments. But this was something new—*the ruler of an empire!*

Some thirty years later Gustl Kubizek and Adolf Hitler met again. Gustl had become a conductor. Adolf had become the dictator of Germany and the conqueror of Austria. Adolf recalled to Gustl what he had prophesied that moonlit night on the Feinberg. "In that hour," Adolf Hitler said to his boyhood friend, "it began."

Life had begun for Adolf Hitler some sixteen years earlier, on April 20, 1889, at the tiny river town of Branau am Inn on the border between Germany and the Austro-Hungarian Empire. Adolf was the fourth child born to Alois and Klara Hitler, but the other three had died in infancy.

Fearful that this baby also might die, Klara coddled him. She was twenty-nine, almost twenty-five years younger than her husband. A docile, plump, pink-cheeked woman, she was her husband's niece. Before their marriage she had worked for him as a housemaid.

Alois Hitler had been married twice previously to women who were now dead. He proudly wore the flashy scarlet uniform of a customs official in the service of the emperor. The equivalent of an army captain, he walked with the iron-spined erectness of a monocled Prussian general. Born on a farm of peasant parents, he liked to boast that he had "become something."

Alois had grown up with the name Alois Schicklgruber. A few years before his marriage to Klara his last name was legally changed to Hitler. A man named Hitler had sworn in court that he was Alois Schicklgruber's true father. That change of name may have changed history. Years later Alois' son, Adolf, would be hailed by millions shouting, "Heil Hitler!" Many historians have doubted whether those same crowds would have shouted, "Heil Schicklgruber!"

Alois' mother had been named Schicklgruber. She was unmarried when she gave birth to Alois, so the baby was given her name. She had worked in the home of a Jewish businessman shortly before Alois was born. Neighbors whispered that the businessman had fathered Alois. If that suspicion was correct—and it has never been proved or disproved—Adolf Hitler, the son of Alois, had a Jewish grandfather and so was part Jewish. Years later this man ordered laws stripping German citizenship from anyone who was even one-eighth Jewish and his killers slaughtered millions of Jews, while Hitler knew all the time that he himself might be part Jewish.

Pompous and stern, Alois Hitler tyrannized his family. He growled that Klara's coddling was making Adolf "a mama's boy." Living with Alois and Klara were a son and daughter, Alois, Jr., and Angela, Alois' children by a previous marriage. Once Alois grabbed his son, Alois, Jr., by the neck and whipped him until he was senseless. Neighbors whispered that Alois beat the family dog until it wet the floor. Klara often hid Adolf and his baby sister, Paula, as her husband stormed through the house, shouting and swearing, while the older Angela and Alois, Jr., cowered in corners.

The swaggering Alois liked to boast of the greatness of the Austro-Hungarian Empire he served as a customs officer. The empire stretched over much of Central Europe from Germany eastward to Russia. Its capital was the glittering city of Vienna. The empire's royal family ruled over a polyglot population of Germans, Austrians, Poles, Czechs, Slavs, Hungarians, Jews, and Turks.

When he was only six, perhaps as a rebellion against his empire-loving father, Adolf began to refer to himself as German rather than Austrian. Once he told a playmate, "You are not a German. You have dark hair and dark eyes." *His* eyes, said Hitler, were blue and his hair brown—the fair complexion of the Teutons, the warriors of ancient Germany.

For a while the Hitler family lived in Passau, on the German side of the border. Adolf played with German children and began to speak with their rolling Bavarian dialect. When the family moved back across the border to Austria, he continued to speak German with that dialect, as he would for the rest of his life. He called it "my mother tongue."

When he was seven, the family settled in a farmhouse outside Linz in Austria. At the Volksschule (elementary school), little Adolf was the brightest student in a class filled mostly with peasant children.

He was the leader of their games. His favorite was cowboys and Indians. Wide-eyed, he read the Wild West stories of Karl May, a German writer who wrote hair-raisers about battles on the faraway American plains. Hitler's favorite hero was Old Shatterhand, a cowboy in May's books who could run a bullet between the eyes of a galloping Indian from half a mile away.

Neighbors called Adolf "the wild boy," whose pants were usually ripped after he had led his cowboys or Indians on raids through orchards of peach trees. Whether he was a cowboy or an Indian, Adolf always was the strutting leader.

At home, though, he was a docile child who worshiped and hugged his mother. Once he delighted her by promising to be a priest. The Hitlers were Roman Catholics, and Adolf served for a while at a nearby monastery as a candle bearer. But one day he was caught smoking by a monk, expelled from service in the monastery, and never again did he show enthusiasm for becoming a priest.

When Adolf was nine, his fourteen-year-old half brother, Alois, escaped from his father's whip by running away. He never returned. Now Adolf caught the full weight of his father's brutalities.

By now Alois Hitler had retired as a customs official. He demanded that Adolf follow in his footsteps as a civil servant of the empire. He showed Adolf the office where he had been a supervisor, checking the passports of travelers. Adolf saw rows of young clerks hunched behind desks, pens in hands, and he thought of caged animals. He swore to friends that he would never be any-one's servant.

After graduating from the country elementary school, Hitler attended a high school in the city of Linz. Now he had to com-pete against city boys. His grades dropped lower and lower. He blamed his teachers. "I would have done better," he told his doting mother, "had not the teacher been a congenital idiot." Others were "absolute tyrants." From those high school days and for the rest of life, Hitler sneered at scholars and intellectuals, who did not understand what "real life in the streets was all about."

Embarrassed by his poor grades, Hitler retreated into a private world of his own where he was a young artist. Sitting at home, he sketched houses, streets, buildings, and bridges. One day a neighbor, visiting his mother, asked him what he was doing. Haughtily the thirteen-year-old Adolf said he was sketching an idea "for one of the new and beautiful buildings that will arise in Linz when I am a famous architect."

The neighbor laughed. Hitler flushed and stalked out of the room. Later he told his mother that he had "no time for low people. They will never understand me. I am destined to fulfill a higher position in the better class of society."

Only one of his teachers made Hitler lean forward, eyes gleam-ing, during a lecture. That was Professor Leopold Poetsch, a thin history teacher who was a devout believer in Pan-Germanism. The Pan-Germanists argued that Germany should gobble up areas of Europe where the majority of the people were former Germans who still spoke German. The minority in that area might not desire to be part of Germany, said the Pan-Germanists, but those minorities were "inferior races" and should be made subject to Germany and Germans.

To demonstrate the "natural and historical" superiority of Germans, Professor Poetsch told Hitler and his other students of the fiery Teuton warriors who had battled Caesar's Roman legions. He spoke of Otto von Bismarck, Germany's nineteenth-century statesman, and how he had unified the states of Germany into a powerful nation under a Kaiser. He described how Germany had humbled France in the Franco-Prussian War of 1870. "How could anyone study German history under such a teacher," Hitler later wrote, "without becoming an enemy of the [Austro-Hungarian] state?"

But in most of his other classes Hitler was a poor student. "He always thinks he is right about everything," one teacher told his worried mother. "He argues with other students in class, even with his teachers. He seems to have no control over his temper."

Another teacher complained that while Hitler seemed to grasp some subjects easily, particularly art and history, he was a lazy worker and a daydreamer.

His father whipped Adolf when he brought home poor grades. After one whipping the father told the crying boy that he would become a civil servant. "Never," Hitler shouted, tears still streaking his face. "I will become a painter and an artist."

"Painter? Artist?" His father was dumbfounded. Painters and artists, to him, were the ragged bums of society, living in dingy garrets. "You will never be an artist!" he roared.

Hitler decided to do what his half brother had done: run away from home. His father caught him and laughed, ridiculing the fourteen-year-old "for not being even able to accomplish a simple thing like running away." He whipped Adolf with a leather lash. Adolf bit his lip, refusing to cry, and he swore he would never again cry in front of his father—and, according to him, he never did.

One morning in January, 1903, Alois Hitler took his usual morning stroll to a nearby coffeehouse. He sat down at a table and keeled over, stricken by a blood clot in the brain. Minutes later he was dead.

His widow and two of her children, Adolf and his baby sister, Paula (Angela, Adolf's half sister, had married), moved from the farmhouse to an apartment building in Linz. The family was well off since Hitler's mother received her husband's full pension from the state.

In the autumn of 1905, when Hitler was sixteen, he convinced his mother that he should drop out of high school so that he could study to be an artist. Always agreeable to his wishes, she gave him all the money he asked for. And so began what he later called "the happiest years of my life, almost a dream."

He awoke late each morning to dress fastidiously in the fashionable clothes of a gentleman. He had grown a small mustache. He brandished an ivory-tipped black cane and wore smooth kid gloves as he sauntered the broad avenues of Linz, imagining himself the carefree gentleman.

He did little studying. He took piano lessons, but soon stopped, bored by practice. He wrote poetry. He sketched buildings and bridges and did impress people with the way he copied the lines of a structure. But when he drew people, they appeared stilted and unreal. When a friend asked him what he was going to do for a living, he said airily that "no bread-and-butter, morning-to-night job" was good enough for him.

He began to attend the opera, where, one evening, he became friendly with Gustl Kubizek. On their nighttime strolls together after the opera, Hitler told his new friend, over and over, of "my beautiful dream of the future as a painter and architect."

Gustl introduced Adolf to his other friends. They thought Hitler strange. He wasn't interested in sports, calling them a waste of time. Instead, he wanted to shout loudly about the problems he said were thrown in the way of ambitious young men trying to rise in the world. Parents and teachers, he ranted, eyes snapping, "lived in the past" and tried to stop the young from "being something."

"He saw everywhere only obstacles and hostility," Gustl once said. "He was always up against something and at odds with the world. . . . He was constantly bringing up new problems that had to be attacked and destroyed."

But Gustl's mother was fascinated by her son's new friend. "Those eyes," she told Gustl, "the way they shine at you. . . ."

One night shortly after their visit to the Feinberg, Hitler told Gustl that he was planning to leave Linz and go to Vienna. He would take the entry tests to enroll at the Academy of Fine Arts, where he would study to be an architect.

His mother cried when Hitler told her of his plans; but he soothed her and she agreed to pay his expenses in Vienna, where he would rent a room. In the fall of 1907, now eighteen, he arrived in Vienna and took the entrance exams for the academy. The results were mailed to him: He had failed.

He was stunned as he stared at the letter of rejection. "I was so confident of my success," he later wrote, "that the announcement of my rejection struck me like a thunderbolt from the clear sky."

Angrily he applied to take the test again the following year. He told himself he would live in Vienna and study on his own, sketching by candlelight in the dingy rented room.

But then he learned from his sister that his mother was ill. She was dying of breast cancer. He went back to Linz and cared for her during the last weeks of her life. Just before Christmas, 1907, she died.

Hitler wept profusely at the graveside during the burial ceremony as a priest read prayers. Afterward Hitler told Gustl, "This was a dreadful blow. I had honored my father. But my mother I loved."

Years later an oil painting of his mother hung over Hitler's desk in his office. There was never one of his father.

A few days after the burial, on a cold and windy January day in 1908, the eighteen-year-old Adolf Hitler trudged down the main street of Linz. He carried a suitcase that contained all his belongings. He was nearly penniless, the pension having stopped with his mother's death. And whatever money had been left in his mother's bank account he left to his half sister, Angela, to care for herself and his younger sister, Paula.

With him as he walked to the railroad station was Gustl. Later Hitler wrote of that leave-taking: "With a suitcase in my hand and an indomitable will in my heart, I set out for Vienna. I too hoped to wrest from fate what my father had accomplished fifty years before. I too hoped to become something—but in no case a civil servant."

Gustl watched the train chug out of the station, billowing clouds of steam. Hitler waved from an open window and shouted, "Follow me soon, Gustl!"

Gustl waved back. He hadn't told Adolf what the dying Klara Hitler had said to him a few days before she died. "Gustl," she had whispered hoarsely, "go on being a good friend to my son when I'm no longer here. He has no one else."

3

"Force, Terror, Violence . . ."

Gustl walked into the room and looked around. Sunlight filtered through a small window. A kerosene lamp stood on a small table in the corner. Two swaybacked beds, with iron posts, filled most of the room. Gustl realized that when he and Adolf were in this room together, one would have to lie on the bed each morning and wait for the other to dress. There wasn't room for two people to stand.

But Gustl smiled at Adolf, who was eyeing him anxiously as the landlady showed them the furnished room. Gustl had arrived in Vienna that morning to join Adolf in this rented room at 29 Stumper Alley, a few blocks from the smoky, noisy railroad station. Gustl said the room was fine. The landlady smiled and left.

"Let me look at you," Gustl said, grasping Adolf by the shoulders. Gustl was overjoyed to be with Adolf, although it had been only a week since Adolf had left Linz, calling for Gustl to follow him. Before leaving Linz, the persuasive Adolf had talked Gustl's father into allowing his son to come to Vienna to study at the Conservatory of Music. Gustl, seeing his stubborn father worn down by Adolf, had come to think that Adolf could convince anybody to do anything.

Looking at Adolf, Gustl saw a thin, mustached eighteen-year-old whose dark hair was now combed down over his forehead. The eyes, he noticed, still had that searching look. "Adolf spoke with his eyes," Gustl once said. "Even when his lips were silent, one knew what he wanted to say."

Gustl didn't know that Hitler had failed the test to enter the Academy of Art. A few days later Gustl took the test for the Conservatory of Music. Within a few days he received a letter notifying him that he had passed.

The excited Gustl told Hitler he had been admitted to the music conservatory. Gustl didn't notice the sharp edge of envy in Hitler's voice as he said bitingly, "I had no idea I had such a clever friend."

Each morning Gustl rose early and went off to his classes. He left Hitler behind, sleeping. Gustl assumed that Hitler rose later to go to his classes at the Academy of Art.

One evening Gustl inquired about Hitler's art studies. Hitler rose from his bed and paced the lane between the beds as Gustl, lying on his bed, watched him curiously.

"Those idiots at the academy know nothing," Hitler was shouting. "They know nothing of true art and are all mental incompetents."

"But, Adolf," Gustl asked, hesitantly, "is it not possible that you must be learning something about drawing and painting?"

Hitler glared down at him. "They rejected me!" he growled. "They turned me down!"

Gustl stared, wide-eyed. He knew how Hitler had put all his hopes into the dream of being an artist. Nothing more terrible could have happened to him, he thought.

Hitler's face was now chalk white. His eyes glittered. For the first time Gustl realized "there was something sinister about them."

Hitler ranted on. ". . . a lot of old-fashioned, fossilized civil servants . . . the whole academy ought to be blown up. . . ."

When Hitler stopped sputtering and stood staring out the dirty window, Gustl asked quietly, "What now?"

Hitler flopped onto his bed and picked up a book. "Never mind," he said, suddenly calm. Later he wrote to a friend to say that the world of art "had lost a great deal" when he had failed to enter the academy. But he added, "Or has fate chosen me for something else?"

Through the spring and summer of 1908 Hitler labored over drawings and sketches he would submit to the academy in the fall, hoping he would be given another entrance exam. Between drawings he started to write an opera. Often he awoke Gustl at three in the morning with a new idea for the opera. But after a few days there was less talk of the opera, and then Hitler stopped talking about it altogether.

The next week he was writing a play. He sat up night after night, head bent to the yellowish light of the kerosene lamp, scribbling on thin sheets of paper. Gustl read the plays. He praised them but noted to himself that the ideas for the plays had been lifted from German mythology.

The plays ended up as curling sheets of paper in the corner of the dingy room. Now Hitler was hunched over drawings for new apartment buildings. "All tenements will be demolished," he told Gustl grandly. His new buildings would rise in their place, he said with a king's decisiveness in his voice. But soon the sketches for the buildings were piled up in the corner with the discarded plays and operas.

In September, 1908, Hitler nervously submitted his drawings

and sketches to the academy. They were quickly returned to him with a curt note that they were not good enough for him to be allowed to take the entrance exam again.

Hitler sat on his bed in the small room, the note crushed in his hands. All his hopes of rising in the world had been put into one balloon: that he would be a great artist. That balloon had been shot down. Now, having crashed with it, Hitler sat stunned.

And he felt humiliated. He could not face Gustl, to whom he had boasted so long about his artistic greatness. Hitler fled the room at 29 Stumper Alley. He left no note for Gustl. They would not meet again for more than thirty years.

Hitler dropped into the underworld of Vienna. He became a ragged, dirty tramp. He slept on benches or in parks. His hair curled down below his neck and looked greasy and dirty. Wearing thin, smelly clothes, he shivered on street corners as he begged for pennies. One day a Hungarian Jew, seeing him look so pitiful, gave him his torn overcoat. Hitler accepted it gratefully, bowing over and over.

For much of the next four years Hitler plodded grimly through a jungle of the poor, the old, the crippled, the demented, a jungle infested with thieves and murderers. He lived in barrackslike buildings for the homeless. Often, at night, he couldn't sleep amid the stench of decaying garbage. Cockroaches crawled the walls. Crowded hallways were filled with the squalling of hungry babies and the screams of half-mad beggars.

"It was the saddest period of my life," he wrote a dozen years later. "Even now I shudder when I think of those pitiful dens, the shelters and lodging houses, those sinister pictures of dirt and repugnant filth. . . ."

One morning, slouched on a cot in a flophouse, Hitler began a conversation with another wanderer. His name was Reinhold Hanisch, a stumpy, bearded former servant. He had traveled to

Germany, and he entranced Hitler with stories of the wonders of that country that Hitler, though an Austrian, called his fatherland.

Hanisch asked Hitler about himself and learned he had been to high school. How, Hanisch asked, could a man with so much education have fallen to a flophouse? Hitler shrugged and said, "I don't know myself."

"What do you do for a living?"

"I am a painter."

"Well, there are many houses to paint. You should make a lot of money."

Hitler drew himself straight and glared. "I am not a house painter. I am an artist."

He showed Hanisch some of his sketches. The quick-witted Hanisch suggested a partnership. "You do as many drawings and paintings as possible. I will sell them," he told Hitler. "We will divide what I bring in fifty-fifty."

Hitler agreed. For the next few days, sitting in a small room of the flophouse, Hitler copied various views of Vienna from picture postcards. He painted watercolors of St. Stephen's Cathedral and the ornate, gilded Parliament Building. In Hitler's drawings the buildings looked real, but the colors were watery. The energetic Hanisch sold them to tourists for the equivalent of a nickel or dime. He went off each morning with several dozen watercolors and came back at night empty-handed, begging Hitler to turn out more. "I can sell them as fast as you paint them," he said excitedly. Each evening, with money now jingling in their pockets, the two partners sat in cafés, suddenly gentlemen of leisure, sipping coffee and reading the papers.

In the mornings Hitler often awoke snarling at Hanisch, who demanded more paintings. "He was never an ardent worker," Hanisch later said. "He was unable to get up in the morning, had difficulty getting started, and seemed to be suffering from a paralysis of the will."

"I must have leisure, I am not a coolie," Hitler snapped when Hanisch nagged him.

But to Hanisch's annoyance, Hitler had the time to argue with other bums in the flophouse about politics. He waved a painting brush or a T square as he lectured to the men on Pan-Germanism, shouting loudly that all Germans should be part of Germany. He looked like a mad orator, his beard long and matted with filth, his hair flopping in front of eyes, his only suit and shirt spotted with stains.

Hitler had begun to read a magazine called *Ostara*. The magazine's writers proclaimed that "blond Aryans," like the Germans and the Scandinavians, "must rule the earth by destroying their dark, racially mixed enemies." The magazine's articles accused Jews of owning all the banks, theaters, and art galleries of Europe. Those lies were swallowed whole by Hitler, for now he could explain to himself why he had been rejected by the academy: It was controlled by Jews who wanted to subjugate an Aryan like himself!

Prowling the streets of Vienna, a shabby figure in his old and tattered clothes and long beard, he saw many Jews and was repelled, he wrote years later. They were "positively repulsive in their long caftans and black hair locks . . . gradually I began to hate them."

Yet in those days he walked the streets with two Jews who slept near him in the flophouse. One was named Josef Neumann and the other was a one-eyed locksmith named Robinson. He told them of his gratitude to Jewish charities that had fed and clothed him. And he talked of a Jewish doctor in Linz who had eased the pain of his dying mother.

In Hitler's mind, however, strange fantasies were taking shape.

So far—both as a teenager in Linz and now as an adult in Vienna —he had never dated a girl. He had never had a girlfriend. He had admired a few women—but only from afar. In Linz he had talked longingly to Gustl about one young woman. He never said a word to her. Years later, to her astonishment, the now-mature woman learned from Gustl that Hitler had talked of leaping off a bridge because she had not returned his love. She had never even seen the now-famous Hitler glance at her, she said. But he had, admiring her and wanting her from the shadows.

In his mind, Hitler began to blame the Jews for the emptiness and the lack of fulfillment in his life. "With satanic joy in his face," he later wrote, "the black-haired Jewish youth lurks in wait for the unsuspecting Aryan girl, whom he defiles with his blood, thus stealing her from her people."

Other ideas were solidifying in Hitler's mind. "In this period," he once claimed, there began to form within him "the granite foundation of all my later acts."

On this "granite foundation," Hitler would build Nazism.

One afternoon he saw a young woman standing on a box and displaying a bottle to a fascinated group of women. What was in this bottle, she told the women, would make them irresistible to men. The women lined up to buy the bottle.

Hitler pushed closer and examined the bottle. He guessed that the bottle was filled with scented water. The stuff was as worthless as any cheap perfume, he told himself, walking away, but he was in awe of the woman's boldness in proclaiming the "magic" of the liquid. "Propaganda! Propaganda!" Hitler shouted that night to the motley group of bums who were often his drunken audience. "You must keep it up until it creates a faith and people no longer know what is imagination and what is reality."

With hundreds of others he stood in squares and listened to the thundering speeches of "Handsome Karl" Lueger, the mayor of Vienna. Lueger assailed "the Jewish bankers who control Vienna" and promised "to do something for the little man."

"The broad masses of the people," Hitler told himself, "can only be moved by the power of speech." And he admired Lueger's trick of giving the mob what it wanted—an enemy, the Jew, it could fix its hate upon.

After a quarrel with Hanisch, Hitler took a job as a day laborer, hauling bricks in a cart to where a building was being erected. Despite his dirty clothes and grimy face, he set himself apart from what he called the "ordinary workers." He later explained, "I drank my bottle of milk and ate my piece of bread off to one side."

One day another worker asked him to join the union. Hitler refused. The next morning two workers grabbed Hitler and put him on a scaffold that was hoisted some hundred feet into the air. With their feet the workers made the scaffold sway. A terrified Hitler begged them to stop. "Join the union tomorrow," a worker told him grimly, "or you'll land on the ground below."

When he was put back onto the ground, Hitler scampered away. He didn't return. But he had learned something. "The weapons which most easily overcome reason are terror and violence," he later wrote. "Only force rules. Force is the first law."

In early 1910 Hitler had his last quarrel with Hanisch. He decided that he would paint his watercolors and sell them himself. The enterprising Hanisch, who had been the first to encourage Hitler as an artist, was told he was no longer needed. Hanisch left the flophouse both angry and bitter. He had steered Hitler off a road that was carrying him to the depths. Hitler repaid him some two decades later—with a bullet in the head.

Hitler began to concentrate on watercolors. His renderings of churches, monuments, and bridges became sharper and almost as lifelike as color photos. When he put people into the paintings, however, they had the stiffness of puppets. But he sold painting after painting to art dealers in Vienna (one was resold in 1976 for $3,000, only because the artist had become so famous).

He was still living in the flophouse, where the other men looked at him with awe as a man of means. Hitler lent money to others who were as desperate as he had been two years earlier. "I saw him several times starting a collection with a hat in his hands," another flophouse inmate later said. ". . . he was good-hearted and helpful."

Over Hitler's bed hung a framed poem: "We look joyously across to the German fatherland/Heil!"

His yearning to see Germany became so strong that he decided to seek success as an artist in Germany. In May, 1913, after five years of what he called "study and suffering in Vienna, the hardest, though most thorough school of my life," he walked to the Vienna railroad station, carrying a single bag, and stepped on a train for Germany.

He carried something else: that granite foundation inside him. "I had set foot in this town while still a boy," he later wrote of Vienna, "and I left it a man, [having] obtained the foundations for a philosophy . . . and a political view which . . . never left me."

In Vienna, "that hardest of schools," a German historian, Joachim C. Fest, has written, Hitler built his "belief in brutal struggle, in harshness, cruelty, destruction, the power of the stronger. . . . He would never forget the lessons he had learned in that school for meanness in Vienna."

On a sunny Sunday morning, May 25, 1913, the twenty-four-year-old Hitler stared from a train window at the green hills of southern Germany. His train clattered into Munich. He walked from the railroad station through the empty streets of a Germany he would one day pull down around him in flame and smoke. He gaped at the stone buildings, "full of enthusiasm," he later wrote, feeling "a deep love for this, a *German* city."

He was still wearing the baggy old clothes of the Vienna flophouse. But he had washed his face and trimmed his beard. He looked like a young artist and had no difficulty finding a room at 34 Schleissheimerstrasse, a building owned by a tailor named Popp. The room, on the third floor, looked down on a cobble-stoned, narrow street. In the room were a bed, table, sofa, and chair. He paid Frau Popp a few marks as a deposit, then walked to a police station, where he registered, a legal requirement for all aliens. He identified himself as "Adolf Hitler, architectural painter from Vienna."

He was still an Austrian citizen. In Vienna he had not reported for military service with the Austro-Hungarian army, which he should have done when he was twenty-one and was no longer a student. He thought the Austrian authorities, like his family, had lost track of him in the Vienna underworld.

Each day Hitler worked in the mornings, then trotted out onto the streets each afternoon with a packet of sketches and paintings under his arms. At first he tried to sell them to art galleries. Doors were slammed in his face. After a while, desperate, he hawked the paintings to men drinking beer at the oak tables in the city's hundreds of beer halls.

He sold a few paintings a week, enough to pay his rent, which was the equivalent of only a few dollars a month. But he could afford to buy only one meal a day, often a bowl of soup and crackers. He was nearly always hungry, and he became so thin he had the stick look of a scarecrow. Herr Popp, his landlord, felt sorry for the skinny "Austrian charmer" and invited him to dine with his family, but Hitler, reluctant now to accept charity, firmly said no.

At nights he sat in beer halls, gripping a single stein of cheap beer, and listened to arguments about politics. Occasionally he would stand up and outshout those who argued that Pan-Germanism would make Germany so bloated with people that the nation would collapse. When he wasn't painting, he read books by German philosophers such as Friedrich Wilhelm Nietzsche, who claimed that "supermen" would one day rule the earth.

On a wintry Sunday afternoon, January 18, 1914, Hitler was reading in his room when he heard a knock on the front door downstairs.

Frau Popp opened the door. She saw a Munich policeman. He asked if there was an Adolf Hitler residing in the building. She said there was. The policeman asked if Herr Hitler could come downstairs.

Frau Popp called upstairs, and Hitler came down. The policeman asked him if he was Adolf Hitler. The gaunt, bearded Hitler said yes.

"You are under arrest," the policeman said.

4

"So It Had Been in Vain"

Hitler nibbled nervously on the pen. He stared at the white sheet of paper. He knew that this was the most important letter he had ever written. Seated in his small room, a kerosene lamp flickering at his elbow. Hitler realized that this letter could decide his future. He could be thrown into a prison cell for years if this letter did not save him.

He was writing the letter a few days after his arrest. The Austrian authorities had tracked him to Munich and ordered his arrest for trying to evade military service in the Austrian army.

The German police had felt sorry for this emaciated, trembling artist. They suggested that he write a letter of apology to the Austrian authorities. The Austrians, they suggested, might withdraw the order for his arrest.

Hitler, biting his lip nervously, began to write. He claimed that he had registered for service with the Austrian army in 1910, four years earlier. His papers, he said, must have been lost by an official in Vienna.

Then he began to beg for sympathy. He told of his hard life in

Vienna and Munich. "I never learned to know the beautiful word 'youth.' Today, after five years, my memories are still in the form of frost-bitten fingers, hands and feet. . . . Despite great need amid my often questionable surroundings, I kept my name clean and am not guilty in the face of the law and have a clear conscience. . . ."

He went on pleading and making excuses. Years later he would write, "Woe to the weak, the strong shall always overpower them." But now he pictured himself as young and weak—and he saved himself. His letter melted the heart of some Austrian official. The order for his arrest was rescinded. He was instructed to report to a town on the Austrian-German border for a physical examination for the armed forces. Hitler reported and was examined. The five-foot-nine, 145-pound Hitler was rejected: "not strong enough to bear arms."

A happy Hitler jumped onto a train that took him back to Munich. "I didn't want to fight for the Austro-Hungarian state," he later explained. "But I was ready to die at any time for Germany."

In Munich he went on painting, walking from door to door selling his pictures. A few months later—the date was June 28, 1914 —he sat at a table in his room, painting. He heard a tumult on the street below. He ran to the stairway. Frau Popp shouted up to him that the Austrian heir, Archduke Franz Ferdinand, had been assassinated.

Hitler ran out into the streets, jammed with people buying newspapers from boys shouting the news. A young Slav terrorist from the small country of Serbia had gunned down the Austrian archduke and his wife on a street. Hitler heard other Germans talking about "the dirty black Slavs" and others predicting grimly that the mighty Austro-Hungarian Empire would revenge the murder of the archduke by wiping little Serbia off the map.

Hitler walked to a nearby beer hall. From his reading of *Ostara*, he—like many Germans—had come to feel contempt and hatred for the Slavs and other "inferior races" of southern Europe. He sat down at a table with a few of his friends. In a slow, measured way, Hitler said, "There will shortly be war."

All across Europe countries took sides—some supporting Austria in its fury at Serbia, others saying they would line up behind Serbia if the small country were attacked by Austria.

During the hot July weeks sweltering Europeans saw bigger and blacker headlines predicting the coming of a great war. Each night European families settled into their beds wondering if they would wake up to the roar of guns. ". . . the sense of the approaching catastrophe [turned] at last to longing," Hitler later wrote. Men, women, and children wanted relief from the growing tension—a relief that could be found with the pulling of triggers and the hurling of bombs.

By late July the two sides had formed for the beginning of World War I. On one side, England, France, Russia, and Italy were lined up against Germany and the Austro-Hungarian Empire on the other side. On August 1 Hitler was one of almost 100,000 people jammed into a square in Munich, cheering the announcement that Germany and the Austro-Hungarian Empire had declared war against Russia. A photographer snapped a picture of that mass of people in the square. Years later, when he was famous, Hitler's face was picked out of that photo and blown up in size. His mouth hung half-open; his eyes seemed to glow with an inner light. "I fell to my knees," he later declared, "and thanked heaven . . . for granting me the good fortune of being allowed to live at this time."

Every nation needed soldiers, even skinny ones. Hitler applied to join the German army and was accepted. He opened the letter of acceptance "with trembling hands," he once said. "My joy and gratitude knew no bounds. Within a few days I was wearing the tunic that I would not take off until almost six years later."

The pasty-faced, thin recruit joined the 16th Bavarian Regiment, named the List Regiment after its commander. He was issued a rifle. "He looked at it," another soldier of the regiment once said, "with the delight that a woman looks at her jewelry."

After years of enduring the hell of the western front, the blinded Hitler was shipped in October, 1918, to a Berlin hospital. There, after treatment, his sight began to be restored. When he read one morning that mutinies were spreading in the German armed forces, he was incredulous. Mutineers should be shot!

A few days later—it was the morning of November 10, 1918— Hitler awoke in his hospital bed and looked out at gray clouds leaden with rain. A nurse came into the ward where Hitler and more than 100 other wounded lay under crisp white sheets. She told them that a minister from a nearby church was coming to the hospital to speak to them.

In an iron-gray hospital robe, Hitler walked with the other soldiers to a large room. Many of the soldiers hobbled on one leg, using canes. Others had lost arms. They were only a few of those who had been wounded, for 2,000,000 Germans had been wounded or killed in the four years of war.

The minister, a white-haired, spare man in his late sixties, walked, head bowed, into the room where the soldiers had gathered. Some sat in wheelchairs, others on the the floor. Hitler saw that the minister was trembling.

He had some bad news, he said. The Kaiser had abdicated and was on his way to exile in Holland. No longer was Germany ruled by an emperor. The new German government—the minister hesitated—was a democracy, like the democracies of the United States and England. The war had been lost. Only a few hours earlier the Germans and Allies had agreed on an armistice—an end to the shooting. At precisely 11 A.M. the next morning, November 11, the war would end. In effect, Germany had surrendered and was ready to sign a treaty of peace. Within a few hours British, French, and American troops would stream into Germany as occupying conquerors.

By now the minister was weeping. So were many of the soldiers. Hitler bolted from the room. "I could stand it no longer," he said later. "It became impossible for me to sit still one minute more."

He had a sudden feeling of dizziness, he said. He staggered down the hallway. "Everything went black before my eyes. I tottered and groped my way back to the dormitory, threw myself on my bunk, and dug my burning head into my blanket and pillows."

Tears streamed down his face. Years later he wrote: ". . . so it had been in vain . . . was it for this that . . . boys of seventeen sank into the earth of Flanders? . . . was it for this that the German soldier has stood fast in the sun's heat and in snowstorms, hungry, thirsty and freezing, weary from sleepless nights and endless marches? Was it for this that he has lain in the hell of the drumfire and in the fever of gas attacks without wavering?"

For days Hitler writhed on the bed, shouting to doctors and nurses that he was blind. One doctor diagnosed his darkening vision as blindness caused by hysteria. Then, gradually, his vision cleared, and after a few days he could see again. But for the rest of his life Hitler had to wear eyeglasses to read (he was so vain he forbade any photographs of himself wearing glasses). And in later life he could read only words printed in very large type.

As his vision became sharper, he said to friends a few years later, so did he see more clearly his own future. "In the days that followed," he once claimed, "my own fate became known to me. I decided to go into politics."

5

"Heads Will Roll—
Ours or Theirs"

The man in the snap-brim fedora and rumpled trench coat strode into the smoky room. He looked around. He saw about forty men, puffing on pipes or sipping beer, seated at long tables. Addressing them was a hulking, mustached speaker whose shouts of "November criminals!" and "traitors!" rang out like pistol shots.

The man in the fedora was Adolf Hitler. He sat down at a table and listened to the speaker. Without knowing it, he had taken his place at the first meeting of what would become his Nazi Party.

Seated a few feet away, in this back room of a beer hall in Munich, was Anton Drexler, a bespectacled, mousy machinist who had organized the German Workers Party. There were only about fifty members. Its treasury held about 7 marks, or $2.

Hundreds of tiny political parties like this had sprung up like weeds across Germany in 1919 and 1920 at the end of the war. Party members argued with each other in beer halls, shot at each other in the streets. The cities of Germany had exploded into battlegrounds. "Red" armies fought to turn Germany into a

Communist state like Russia. "White" armies battled to bring back the Kaiser and restore Germany to the monarchy it had been before the war. Each day hundreds of corpses were pulled out of rivers while the leaders of the German democratic government—called the Weimar Republic—tried desperately to keep the Reds and Whites apart.

The leaders of the democracy were assailed by both Reds and Whites as "traitors" and "November criminals." They were accused of having handed over Germany to the Allies on November 11, 1918, and then of having surrendered German wealth and arms to the Allies by signing, in 1919, the Treaty of Versailles, which formally ended World War I. The November criminals, claimed the Reds and Whites, had "stabbed Germany in the back." Both Reds and Whites ignored the truth: that German generals had admitted that the war was lost and further struggle hopeless.

Hitler was still in the army. Assigned to a barracks in Munich, he had sided with the Whites when Communist Red soldiers mutinied and tried to overwhelm the regiment. The Reds were surrounded, captured, and marched off to prison. Hitler went to an officer and pointed out several soldiers who had lined up with the Reds during the mutiny. The officer ordered that the soldiers be marched to a nearby wall, lined up, and shot by a firing squad.

Later another officer heard Hitler speaking to fellow soldiers on his favorite subjects—the menace of Communists and the Jews. He assigned Hitler to be a political instructor, lecturing to soldiers on what the army officers wanted them to be told: that in a choice among communism, monarchy, and democracy, a monarchy was best for Germany.

As part of his job, Hitler attended meetings of political parties. On this night in September, 1919, he had dropped in on a meeting of Anton Drexler's German Workers Party to see if it was strong

50

enough to aid the Reds. After listening to a dull speech, seeing only this handful of beer-drinking workers, Hitler decided this party would soon vanish.

He rose to leave. As he did, a man stood up and began to argue that South Germany should secede from North Germany. That proposal—the breakup of his beloved fatherland—infuriated Hitler. In ringing, biting phrases, he poured ridicule on the man who made the suggestion, and the man, he later claimed, "slunk out of the room like a wet poodle."

Staring, mouth agape, was Anton Drexler. "Man, this one can speak," the founder of the German Workers Party whispered to a fellow member. "He has a big mouth. We can use him."

He looked more closely at the ranting Hitler. He saw a pale, thin face, a crop of brown hair hanging low over his forehead, a thin mustache, and glowing blue eyes. When Hitler finished, breathing heavily, and started to leave, Drexler jumped up and pressed a pink-covered booklet into his hands.

The next morning Hitler awoke in his barracks room at about five in the morning. He scattered pieces of bread around his cot and watched mice scurry out of the corners to nibble at the crumbs. "I had known so much poverty in my life," he once re-called of that moment, "that I was well able to imagine the hunger and, hence, also the pleasure of the little creatures."

Lying on his cot, Hitler picked up the booklet given to him by Drexler. On the pink cover was the title, *My Political Awakening,* by Anton Drexler. As he thumbed the pages, at first quickly and then more slowly, Hitler's eyes widened. Here were ideas that he had often expressed: the need for a strong and united German state, workers and soldiers banding together to stop the Reds.

A few days later Hitler received a postcard. It was an invitation from Drexler to join his German Workers Party. "I didn't know whether to be angry or to laugh," he later said. "The party was so pitifully small and weak." But during the next few days he kept asking himself what this party might do for the future of Adolf Hitler. He sensed that he was strong enough to grab the steering wheel of the party away from Drexler.

Hitler joined the party as its fifty-sixth card-carrying member. "At all costs," he told Drexler, "we have to make the party known." Back at his barracks, hunched over an army typewriter, he pecked out invitations to the next meeting and addressed them to people he had met at Munich political meetings. He walked from house to house, stuffing the invitations in mailboxes. A few nights later he watched, dejected, as only seven new faces appeared for the meeting.

He paid for an ad in a newspaper announcing the next meeting. To his smiling delight, some 100 people crowded into the small back room of the beer hall. Hitler rose at the meeting to make his first public speech. At first speaking slowly and hesitantly, he stumbled over his words. But then he began to pick up speed. Soon he was shrieking warnings that "Red squads of butchers" would burst into German homes and slaughter German men, women, and children. His hair falling down in front of his eyes, his forehead glistening with sweat, he swept up his audience and carried them with him. At times they seemed to be hypnotized by his waving hands, and when he shouted, "Germany must be free!" they roared, and when he ended his speech with a thunderous "Awake, Germany!" men stood and pounded beer steins on the tables.

Groggy from his effort, his shirt soaked, Hitler trudged slowly back to his barracks through the dark streets. He wore a triumphant smile. Over and over again he told himself, "I could speak! I could speak!" He was more than a barracks loudmouth; he was a political orator who could cast a spell over an audience and change it into a loyal pack of people who would trail enthusiastically at his heels.

By 1920 his fiery, shrieking speeches had made him one of Munich's best-known men. "Threatening and beseeching, with small pleading hands and flaming, steel-blue eyes, he had the look of a fanatic," one listener later wrote. "Leaning from the rostrum as though he were trying to inject his inner self into the minds of his thousands of listeners, he was holding the masses and me under a hypnotic spell by the sheer force of his convictions. . . . His words were like a lash. When he spoke of the disgrace of Germany, I felt ready to spring on any enemy. . . . I forgot everything but the man; then, glancing around, I saw that his magnetism was holding these thousands as one."

To this listener—and thousands like him—Hitler was the new leader come to scatter Germany's enemies. Germans could march behind this leader with heads held high, memories of their humiliating defeat and surrender wiped out by new victories.

In speech after speech Hitler demanded the tearing up of the Treaty of Versailles. Germans, he cried, should own colonies in Asia and Africa, where they could live and become rich. And he acted as a loudspeaker that blared out the hatred within many of his listeners when he declared, "No Jew can be a member of the nation!"

By 1922 he was called the King of Munich because so many people surrounded him during his speeches. He had elbowed aside Drexler and was now the party boss. Membership had climbed to more than 6,000. Money from dues filled the treasury. Hitler had resigned from the army. As party leader he paid himself about $50 a week. He drove a fancy sports car. But he still wore his rumpled, belted trench coat and the wide-brimmed fedora snapped over his forehead. He packed a revolver at his hip. When he walked toward a speaker's platform, a dog whip was usually looped around his wrist. Waving the whip, he shouted to audiences that he would "do what Christ did—drive out the Jewish money changers!"

He had changed the party's name. He called the party the National Socialist German Workers Party, in German *Nationalsozialistische Deutsche Arbeiterpartei.* Its initials were NSDAP, which was shortened by Germans to "Nazi," a common Bavarian nickname for Ignatius. Hitler was delighted; the Nazi nickname made the party stand out from the hundreds of others.

To make the Nazis even easier to identify, he designed a new flag. Its background was blood-red. In the middle of the red was a white disk. A black hooked cross, known as a swastika, was imprinted on the white disk.

"In red we see the socialist or workers idea of the movement," he told audiences. "In white there is the nationalist idea, for red, white, and black were the colors of the imperial Germany of the Kaiser. And in the swastika we see the struggle for the victory of the Aryan man."

Hitler had borrowed the swastika from the Thule group, an anti-Semitic organization of former German soldiers who had seen the swastika while fighting during World War I in Finland. The swastika had been worn by Teutonic warriors of ancient Germany. It had also been drawn on the caves of American Indians. To ancient man the hooked cross symbolized the sun's rising, crossing of the sky, and setting. But after Hitler and the Nazis, the swastika would possess a darker and more ominous meaning.

Occasionally Hitler, now a celebrity in Munich and the state of Bavaria, bumped into someone who had known him when he was a tattered beggar in Vienna. He pleaded with them not to tell what they had known of the King of Munich only ten years earlier.

His fame made him a sought-after guest at the parties of Munich's wealthy families. At one of those parties he met the monocled General Erich Ludendorff, one of the country's war heroes who had vanquished the Russian army. The former corporal acted like a frightened schoolboy in the presence of the famous general. As Ludendorff talked, Hitler bowed slightly, tilting his backside after each of the general's sentences, saying respectfully, "Quite so, your Excellency."

But Hitler was the tough leader with the henchmen he had gathered around him. One was Ernst Roehm, a squat, barrel-chested army captain with the blunt face of a bullet. Part of his nose had been shot off during the war, and his face was scarred by the wounds of duels. Roehm swaggered through the streets at the head of bands of Nazi thugs. They wore brown shirts. The official name of the brownshirts was the *Sturmabteilung*, or SA, but they soon became known as Hitler's storm troopers.

Most were tough, hungry, out-of-work war veterans. Often drunk, they roamed the streets of Munich, beating anyone they suspected of being a Communist or a Jew. Late at night Munichers cowered in their homes as the storm troopers paraded by, chanting:

> The Red brood, beat them to a pulp!
> Storm troopers are on the march—clear the way!

At genteel parties, Hitler told society ladies and gentlemen: "Call the brownshirts callous brutes if you want. But if we save Germany, we will have carried out the greatest deed in the world."

And to the cheering storm troopers he shouted, "We will brawl our way to greatness." In directives to Roehm, he stated, "People need a good scare. What is this rot about violence and how shocked people are about torture? The masses want that. They need something to dread."

When Hitler appeared before his storm troopers, they hailed him with chants of "Heil!" and "Heil Hitler!" They saluted him with right arms shooting out at forty-five-degree angles to their bodies, a copy of the salute that Fascists in Italy were now flashing at their strutting, balding leader, Benito Mussolini. Often, with a salute, Nazis shouted, "Heil Hitler!" at each other when they met on a street corner or at a Nazi meeting. And they had begun to call Hitler the Fuehrer, which in German means leader or guide.

One of the new Fuehrer's chief lieutenants was a young and handsome war hero, Hermann Goering. He had been a fighter pilot with Baron Manfrecl von Richthofen's Flying Circus air squadron during the war. Goering had shot down thirty Allied fighter planes in dogfights over France and Germany. After the war he had become an airline pilot and married a beautiful and rich Swedish baroness.

Goering donated some of his wife's millions to the Nazi Party. He introduced Hitler to many of his rich friends. With money from them, Hitler bought a daily newspaper. Now he could trumpet his propaganda to an even bigger audience. The paper's writers attacked Jews with murderous threats that not even Hitler, in his speeches, had dared to use. The newspaper urged the "sweeping out of the Jewish vermin with an iron broom." And it wrote of a "final solution" to the Jewish question, a solution that would be found years later at places like the death camps of Buchenwald and Dachau.

Despite Hitler's fame and the increasing numbers of Germans flooding into the party—it had grown to 10,000 by 1923—many Germans smiled when they talked of Hitler. He was just a comic "drummer" or salesman, they said, and they talked about how he looked like that slapstick actor in the silent movies of the time—Charlie Chaplin.

One day in early 1923 a roving band of storm troopers beat and severely injured a number of Jews. Hitler was charged with inspiring violence and put into jail for a week. He was let go. But, because he was an Austrian alien, he could now be deported from Germany for having been arrested. One vote, by a Socialist leader, would have put Hitler on a train to Austria, where he might have disappeared from sight, remembered only as another flash-in-the-pan crackpot. But the Socialist leader, whose party Hitler had vowed to destroy, voted no instead of yes, and Hitler was allowed to stay in Germany. "Hitler," said the Socialist leader, underestimating him as so many world leaders would also underestimate him, "is a harmless nut."

By 1923 Hitler—more and more confident after his sudden rise to fame—decided it was time for the Nazis to take over Germany as Mussolini's Fascists had taken over Italy. Germans were raising their fists in anger at the shaky postwar democracy that was trying to rule Germany. Inflation had wiped out the savings of millions of people. In 1921, 75 marks had been worth $1. By early 1923, 18,000 marks were the equal of $1. By the summer of 1923 one needed 1,000,000 marks to own the equal of $1.

People came to stores pushing carts filled to overflowing with marks to buy a loaf of bread and a bottle of milk. Prices changed by the hour. In the morning 1,000,000 marks might buy a sandwich; by nightfall the same sandwich sold for 2,000,000 marks.

Germans who had worked lifetimes to save a few thousand marks now, suddenly, were poor. Their savings would not buy a few sticks of matches. Hundreds of people committed suicide. Men walked the streets with stricken looks on their faces, hearing in their minds the crying of their hungry children.

"It can't go on like this," they told each other. "Something has to be done."

Hitler sat down with Goering and Roehm. He told them he would march at the head of a column of storm troopers. First they would take over Munich, the capital of the state of Bavaria.

Then they would march to Berlin, throw the leaders of the democracy out of their offices, and take over as the rulers of Germany.

Goering was appalled. Most of the Nazi Party members, he pointed out to Hitler, were in Munich. The party was unknown in North Germany. The German army would stop any march on Berlin and throw its leaders into prison.

Hitler, buoyed by all those shouts of "Heil Hitler" and his fame as the King of Munich, waved aside Goering's objections. What that strutting Mussolini had done in Italy, he—the King of Munich—could do in Germany.

"I will follow my star!" he shouted. But minutes later his mood had swung downward to somber concern. All his life his moods had soared and dipped like a roller coaster, and now those rises and falls had become steeper. "If I should fail," he somberly told Goering and Roehm, "it would only be a sign that my star has run its course and my mission is fulfilled."

He grinned. "In the coming battle," he said, "heads will roll—ours or theirs."

6

"Revolution!"

The trucks lurched to a squealing stop. Steel-helmeted storm troopers leaped off the trucks amid the glare of headlights, gripping rifles, and rushed by the startled policemen who had been guarding the doors of the beer hall. The storm troopers crowded into the long hallway of the beer hall.

Behind them, gripping a machine pistol, pushed Hermann Goering. He turned and waved to a storm trooper behind him. "Wheel in the machine gun!" he snapped. "Quickly!"

A heavy machine gun was rolled through the doors and down the hallway. It stopped at a swinging door. Goering threw open the door and stalked into the cavernous main hall, filled with more than 3,000 men and women, who were listening to a speaker standing on a stage in the middle of the hall.

Gold earrings and heavy jewelry glittered from the women, many dressed in long evening gowns. Most of the men wore tuxedos and high starched collars. These were the richest industrialists, businessmen, bankers, and lawyers of southern Germany.

They were listening to a speech by the squat, short-legged Dr. Gustav von Kahr, the commissar of the state of Bavaria. He was telling them that despite the ruinous inflation of the past year, Bavaria would survive as part of a growing and healthy Germany. Next to Kahr sat slender, monocled General Otto von Lossow, the commanding general of all the German army (Reichswehr) troops in Bavaria. On Lossow's left sat the stiff-backed, plump Colonel Hans von Seisser, who was the chief of police in Bavaria.

These three—the commissar, the general, the police chief—ruled Bavaria. A few weeks earlier Hitler had promised this ruling triumvirate that he and his Nazis would not attempt a *putsch*—a takeover of the government offices at the point of a bayonet. But Hitler suspected that the triumvirate planned to withdraw the state of Bavaria from the democratic republic that ruled Germans. Then, Hitler also feared, the triumvirate would stamp out the Nazi Party. On this cold night of November 8, 1923, Hitler planned to seize the triumvirate (he knew the three would be onstage at this dinner meeting in the beer hall). With words or with guns he hoped to persuade them to line up alongside him and his Nazis in a march on Berlin to overthrow the republic.

Standing on the stage, Commissar Kahr suddenly stopped speaking. He was staring at the open doorway where Goering stood, pistol in hand. The ugly black snout of a machine gun was pointed directly at Kahr's chest. The crowd turned to see what he was looking at. They saw Goering and the rifles and the helmets of the storm troopers, and then they saw the machine gun.

Women screamed. Steins of beer crashed off the tables. Men jumped on the tables to see above the commotion. Men and women poured into the aisles between the tables, pushing toward doors to get out of the hall.

Through the crowd pushed Hitler, flanked by a beefy body-guard, who shoved aside men and women with his fists and elbows. The King of Munich was wearing a black evening suit and a glistening white shirt. Some, not recognizing him, thought he was a waiter. His face was chalk white and sweaty. In one hand he waved a pistol.

"Quiet! Quiet!" he shouted into the pandemonium. He jumped onto a chair, thrust the pistol into the air, and fired a shot at the ceiling.

The sudden explosion shocked the screaming people. There was a sudden hush. Hitler, led by his bodyguard, scrambled over tables, then climbed onto the stage. He pushed by the glaring triumvirate and shouted, his voice shaky, into the microphone: "The National Revolution has broken out! The hall is surrounded by six hundred heavily armed men. No one may leave it!"

Men stood on tables and shouted at him: "Madman! Traitor!"

"Unless quiet is restored immediately," Hitler shot back, his voice steadying, "I shall have a machine gun placed in the gallery."

Again the hall quieted, and Hitler went on: "The Bavarian government and the national government have been overthrown. The barracks of the Reichswehr and the state police have been occupied. The Reichswehr and the state police are already advancing under the banner of the swastika."

The army and the state police were not advancing under the swastika. They didn't even know what was happening at this beer hall. But by a big lie, Hitler hoped to trick the triumvirate into thinking they had to join him or face troops and police who had turned against them.

Pointing his pistol at the triumvirate, Hitler ordered the leaders to follow him to a room on the edge of the stage. Inside, he slammed shut the door. He picked up a stein of beer and swallowed half of it in several long gulps. Hitler seldom drank beer, but now he seemed to need any courage it could give him. His face was still white and moist with sweat.

The plump Colonel Seisser reminded Hitler of his recent promise: that he would not attempt a putsch.

Hitler flushed. With a slight bow, he said, "I did it for the good of Germany. Forgive me."

Then he seemed to brace himself. He drew erect. He warned the three not to speak to one another. "You will be shot immediately if you do," he growled. Behind them stood two storm troopers, rifles in their hands.

Kahr sensed that Hitler was unsure of himself. "Herr Hitler," he said, adjusting his monocle, "you can have me shot or shoot me yourself. Whether I die or not is no matter."

Hitler became calmer. He proposed that they join with him in separating the state of Bavaria from the republic in Berlin. Hitler would be the head of a "temporary" Bavarian government until the arrival of a new King of Bavaria from the family of the exiled Kaiser Wilhelm.

The three stood silent. If they refused, Hitler warned, waving the pistol, they would die. "I have four bullets in my pistol," he said menacingly. "Three for you, my colleagues, if you fail me. The last one for myself."

The three still said nothing. Hitler switched to flattery. "The people of Germany," he said, "will kneel before you."

Kahr said, dryly, that things like that meant nothing to him. He wanted to be no king of Munich.

An ominous silence hung in the room for several moments. Then, through the door, burst General Ludendorff, the hero of Tannenberg, the battle that had destroyed the Russians. Hitler's aides had brought Lundendorff to the beer hall at Hitler's orders. Hitler hoped that the old war hero could sway the triumvirate into joining with his Nazis.

Dressed nattily in a tweed jacket and blue pants, the old general shouted that he had known nothing of Hitler's putsch.

He was angry. A putsch that began in a beer hall! This was too much to expect—even from these brawling Nazis.

Facing the triumvirate, his back to Hitler, the feisty Ludendorff, fists clenched, told them he was shocked by the putsch. Hitler fidgeted, staring at the floor, his pale cheeks flushing with red dots of embarrassment.

Ludendorff paused, his back still to Hitler. And yet, he told the triumvirate, there probably would be no better time than now to overthrow this detestable republic. Ruined by inflation, millions of Germans were straining for a change. They would throw their weight behind a blow at the republic and follow the Nazis, who had been chanting for weeks, "On to Berlin!"

Hitler bowed deferentially toward Ludendorff. His Excellency was correct. In any case the putsch could no longer be stopped. Already his storm troopers were arresting leaders of the Bavarian government. Others were maching on army barracks. "There is no turning back," he said, his scratchy voice betraying his quivering nerves.

Ludendorff ignored Hitler. Still facing the three leaders, he said, "All right, gentlemen. Come along with us and give me your hand on it."

General Lossow and Colonel Seisser shook hands with Ludendorff. But Kahr, the politician, held back his hand. He was not eager to see Hitler above him as the head of a new government. He snapped that a king should rule Bavaria. Hitler quickly replied that this, too, was his intention. Kahr finally put out his hand and shook Ludendorff's.

A beaming Hitler led the foursome back onto the stage. As Hitler approached the microphone, a wave of boos rolled at him. The crowd had grown mutinous in the smoky heat of the beer hall, its door shut tight by the storm troopers.

Hitler ignored the taunts and insults thrown at him as he began to speak. He pointed out Ludendorff, standing on the stage. The crowd, recognizing the old war hero, cheered. Hitler told them that Ludendroff would lead a new German army, and the crowd cheered again.

Pointing to the triumvirate, Hitler said they would join with him as the heads of a new, temporary Bavarian government. Again the crowd roared, suddenly sensing it was attending a historic moment: the birth of a new German state.

"This mission of the new regime," Hitler thundered, his raspy voice cutting through the smoke, "is to begin the march on Berlin. . . ."

A wave of new roaring filled the hall, men and women clapping hands, their eyes lit with excitement. "Hitler," a listener later said, "turned the mood of the crowd inside out, like a glove."

Hitler's voice raced on, his body swaying back and forth, the crowd seeming to be magnetized to his words: "I want now to fulfill the vow that I made to myself five years ago, when I was a blind cripple in the military hospital. I will know neither rest nor peace until the November criminals are overthrown, until on the ruins of the wretched Germany of today there has arisen once more a Germany of power and greatness, of freedom and glory . . . amen!"

That last word, flying out like a thunderbolt over the audience, brought people to their feet, cheering, applauding, even weeping. Men and women stretched their right arms in the Nazi salute, and the cry of "Heil! Heil! Heil!" shook the wooden walls of the beer hall. The doors were flung open by the storm troopers. Men and women streamed out into the cold November night, a light snow beginning to fall through a fog. Arms locked together, men and women sang "Germany over All."

Truck loads of storm troopers, meanwhile, swayed through dark Munich streets. The storm troopers smashed into Communist newspaper offices. They flung typewriters out of windows and hammered apart printing presses. Other brownshirts pounded at the doors of Jews and of Nazi opponents. Men were dragged from their homes and beaten. Several were tied to trees and told they would be hanged. This was the first time—it would not be the last—when the "midnight knocking" of Nazi fists on doors would make for terror-filled nights in Germany.

Led by Captain Ernst Roehm, some 400 helmeted storm troopers, armed with rifles and machine pistols, stormed into the nearly deserted German army headquarters in downtown Munich. One of the storm troopers peered nearsightedly through thick glasses. His name was Heinrich Himmler. Himmler and the other brownshirts strung barbed wire around the building, then poked rifles and machine guns through open windows to await a counterattack by the army troops at dawn.

Back at the beer hall Hitler listened to reports from messengers. He was told that army troops at an ammunition depot were firing back at attacking storm troopers. Hitler decided to go to the depot to try to talk the soldiers into surrendering.

It was a fatal mistake.

When Hitler left, the naïve Ludendorff dismissed the riflemen who had been guarding the triumvirate. The old general, a gentleman of the old school, had shaken hands with the three officials. He was sure they would not go back on their word. But the triumvirate immediately raced to their homes and offices, where they assured associates that they hadn't joined Hitler. He had been "putting on an act," explained General Lossow, when he stood on the stage with Hitler. The wily Kahr issued orders that all promises "extorted" from the triumvirate by Hitler were "null and void." He sent a message by teletype to Berlin that Hitler's rebels were massing to march on the capital.

Hitler returned to the beer hall, having been unable to stop the firing by the army troops. He looked around. Where was the triumvirate? he asked Ludendorff. He stared, dumbfounded, when told the triumvirate apparently had left.

A worried Hitler wondered aloud: Would the triumvirate go back on its word to support his putsch?

Ludendorff scowled. "I forbid you," snapped the former general to the former corporal, "to doubt the word of honor of a German officer."

But as dawn came and a wet snow fell softly on a gray Munich, Ludendorff and Hitler gradually realized that the triumvirate had gone over to the government's side. Lossow's army troops and Seisser's state police were pouring into the city, towing cannons and machine guns, and several thousand Reichswehr soldiers had ringed Roehm's storm troopers in the army headquarters.

Slumped on a chair in the empty beer hall, Hitler once more rode the emotional roller coaster from elation to gloom. "If it comes out all right, well and good," he told Goering, his face lined with fatigue after being awake all night. "If not, we'll hang ourselves."

By now, all over the world, people were reading about Adolf Hitler and his small army of rebel Nazis. In New York City subway riders read on the front page of the *Times:* "Adolf Hitler's troops have begun an offensive movement toward Berlin."

In Berlin the ramroad-straight commander in chief of the army sardonically told an aide: "I am no longer head of the armed forces. . . . Hitler is Reich Chancellor, Ludendorff is Defense Minister." Then he shot off a telegram to General Lossow in Munich: "Stop Hitler. If you don't, I will."

At the beer hall Hitler stared glumly out the window at the swirling snow. He was surrounded by some of his chief lieutenants. Goering suggested that the Nazis retreat to the small villages of southern Bavaria, where the party had many supporters. The storm troopers could split into small bands, then hide out in the hills, fighting guerrilla battles against the army troops.

Ludendorff said no. That would only mean a long civil war, he said, that would sap the strength of the antigovernment side. The old general stood up, straight as an arrow. He looked at the shaken, pale Hitler. "*Wir marschieren!*" he snapped. "*We march!*"

Hitler leaped up, excited, eyes aglow. "Yes!" he shouted. With Ludendorff and Hitler, who were so popular, at the head of a column of storm troopers, he said, the army and the police would not dare shoot. The column would be joined, as it marched into Munich, by thousands of people, like those at the beer hall last night. They would occupy the offices of the Bavarian government without firing a shot.

By near noon some 3,000 storm troopers had been assembled in front of the beer hall, located across a river from Munich. The storm troopers lined up in a ragged column. Their faces were dirty and dark with day-old beards. Their brown uniforms were ragged and torn. "We looked," Hitler said years later, "like a bunch of men from the workhouse." The storm troopers carried rifles and machine pistols, but Hitler ordered that the weapons be emptied of bullets. He wanted no firing that would bring a return fire from the heavily armed troops and police.

A few Jews had been roped together and put into the column. Goering wanted to make them march with the column, using them as hostages whose lives could be threatened if the police and army began to fire. But Hitler ordered them to be released. He wanted no dead Jews who could be shown to Germany as martyrs.

His mood once more was low as a trumpet blew and a small band began to play the "Badenweiler March," Hitler's favorite. The column snaked raggedly toward the bridge that led into

Munich. At the head of the column, walking next to Ludendorff, Hitler suggested that perhaps the march be stopped. "We could be gunned down," he whispered to Ludendorff.

The general turned and stared coldly at Hitler. "*Wir marschieren!*" he growled.

7

"Only a Miracle Can Save Him"

The long brown column of Nazis flowed toward the Ludwig Bridge, which spanned the Isar River. At the head of the column trotted eight scouts, armed with rifles. Behind them strode four flag bearers, the swastikas flapping in the whipping November wind. And behind them, eight abreast, marched the Nazi leaders. In the middle was Hitler, his face pale, his trench coat buckled at the waist, its collar pulled high to shield his face from the wind. On his left walked General Ludendorff, on his right a lanky Nazi named Max Erwin von Scheubner-Richter. Also on the front line strode the burly Ulrich Graf, a former butcher who was Hitler's personal bodyguard, and the swaggering Hermann Goering, wearing a black leather coat and a steel helmet.

Spectators lined the curbs, watching the column of marching men. The Nazis were singing their marching song, "Swastika on Helmet," their voices echoing in the cold air.

> Armband black-white-red
> Storm Detachment Hitler
> Is our name . . . .

Among the marchers was the nearsighted storm trooper Heinrich Himmler, peering through his thick glasses. A former chicken farmer and clerk, he believed that Hitler would save him and Germany from a lifetime of poverty. Walking near Himmler was a thick-browed, black-haired, scowling man who looked like a thug but who spoke with the suave tones of a college professor. His name was Rudolf Hess. He had heard one speech of Hitler's and now wrote booklets for the party extolling Hitler as "the new Jesus Christ come to save the world from Jewry and Marxism."

As the first Nazis stepped onto the Ludwig Bridge, they could see a knot of Colonel Seisser's green-uniformed police banded together on the other side. The Green Police, as they were called, were aiming rifles at the advancing column. "Things look ugly," Scheubner-Richter said, fixing his pince-nez glasses, and then he predicted to Hitler—accurately as it turned out—that this would be their last walk together.

As the head of the column approached the Green Police, an order was barked at the Nazis: Stop. The Nazis stopped. One shouted, "Don't shoot at your comrades! Seisser is on our side, and so are his police."

The Green Police glanced uncertainly at their commander. Their rifles drooped. A trumpet blared from the middle of the column: the command to charge. The Nazis rushed at the police, ripping the rifles from their hands. The policemen were overwhelmed, grabbed, then hustled, kicked, and cursed toward the rear of the column.

Cheering, the column swept off the bridge and swaggered, still singing, through the narrow streets of ancient Munich. By now, the time a little after noon on a cold and windy day, thousands jammed the sidewalks to watch the Nazis, wondering whether this line of tough-looking men really would overwhelm the police and army troops. The column streamed into St. Mary's Plaza, the center of the old city, and the storm troopers cheered as they saw the flagpole atop City Hall. The flag of the republic was being run down, the red, black, and white swastika run up.

Leading the column, Ludendorff seemed to take a willy-nilly course, he and Hitler unsure where they were headed. With hundreds of spectators now at its tail, the column, still eight abreast, wormed out of the plaza. The head of the column pushed through a narrow street, the Nazis' singing echoing against the stone walls of government buildings that rose canyonlike on each side of the street.

The street emptied out into another plaza. Blocking the way to the plaza stood another band of Green Police. Their guns were pointed at the chests of the singing Nazis surging toward them.

Hitler nervously locked his left arm into the right arm of Scheubner-Richter. Behind them floated the singing of the column and the trailing spectators, "O Germany, high in heaven. . . ."

The Nazis closed to within a few feet of the pointed bayonets and guns of the Green Police. "No shooting," Ulrich Graf shouted at the police, "General von Ludendorff is coming!"

Two of the Nazis scouts came face to face with Lieutenant Michael von Godin, the burly commander of the police detachment. One scout jabbed a bayonet toward Godin. Godin grabbed a carbine from one of his men and parried the bayonet. Amid the ringing sounds of clashing metal, a gun suddenly barked. A Nazi had disobeyed Hitler's order not to load his gun. His bullet whizzed past Godin's head and plowed into the face of a sergeant standing behind him. Blood spurting from a smashed face, the sergeant dropped, dead.

That shot set off burst after burst of rapid fire from the police. A wave of bullets streamed into the Nazis squeezed shoulder to shoulder in the narrow street.

One bullet struck Scheubner-Richter in the chest, and he fell,

71

his lungs torn open, coughing blood as he died on the pavement. His arm locked with Hitler's, he jerked his Fuehrer toward the ground, the wrench so sudden and violent that Hitler's left arm was dislocated. Hitler felt a numbing pain tear through the shoulder and thought he was shot. His chunky bodyguard, Graf, leaped in front of the fallen Hitler and was riddled by half a dozen bullets that would have killed Hitler. Instead, they killed Graf, who dropped atop the dying Scheubner-Richter.

Behind them men flattened to the pavement to duck that sheet of fire. Amid the roar of guns, someone shouted that Hitler and Ludendorff were dead. When the firing suddenly stopped, storm troopers rose and scampered for safety, begging store merchants and homeowners to hide them in their buildings. Others fled out of Munich, burying their guns and uniforms in the forests.

On the narrow street 16 Nazis were sprawled, dead or dying. Three police were dead. More than 100 Nazis crawled away wounded, blood splotching their clothes. One of the wounded was Hermann Goering, his thigh gashed wide by a bullet. His wound was patched by the wife of a Jewish banker, and then he limped to an automobile. His wealthy wife drove him at 100 miles an hour across the border to Switzerland.

Only one man stood to face the police when the shooting stopped. That was General Ludendorff, the hero of Tannenberg. Walking erectly, one hand thrust defiantly into the pocket of his tweed jacket, he strode toward the smoking guns of the police.

No one fired as he walked by the guns. A policeman stepped in front of him. "Excellency," the policeman said respectfully, "I must take you into protective custody."

"You have your orders," the old general said stiffly. "I will follow you."

While Ludendorff was being led away, Hitler had risen from the pavement. He saw that Graf and Scheubner-Richter were dead. He crawled back toward the rear of the column, gripping his aching left shoulder, still thinking he had been shot. Grimacing with pain, he ran, bent over, until he arrived at St. Mary's Plaza, where a Nazi, driving a car, recognized him. Hitler climbed into the car, and it sped out of Munich and raced south, dust billowing behind it, headed for the mountain home of a woman Nazi sympathizer.

Two hours later General Lossow phoned Commissar Kahr. "Excellency," said Lossow, triumph in his voice, "the Ludendorff-Hitler putsch has been broken."

Commissar Kahr had to smile. He had seemed to have joined that putsch some 18 hours earlier, having given his hand to Ludendorff. But he had slipped away from that disastrous putsch with clever footwork. But one day Hitler would extract a heavy bill from Kahr for what Hitler considered treachery.

During the next two days Hitler hid out from searching police in the attic of the mountain home of his friend. His dislocated arm had been put in a sling, but he was still in pain, as much mental as physical. Deep in one of his depressed moods, he swore he would kill himself. Several times he picked up a pistol and said he would shoot himself. "A man doesn't deserve to live who is responsible for so great a fiasco as I am," he said despondently.

Late in the evening of Hitler's second day as a fugitive, police banged at the door. They swarmed upstairs and found him hiding in the attic. He was gripping a gun in his right hand. He swung the gun toward his head, but he moved awkwardly—perhaps because his left arm was in a sling, perhaps because he had changed his mind about killing himself—and the police easily disarmed him.

Manacled, he was taken to prison. To visitors he said he feared he would be shot by a firing squad. He promised he would starve himself to death rather than face the ignominy of execution. At least a half dozen times during these frantic twenty-four hours he had talked of killing himself.

Most of Germany and the world sighed with relief at the news that the putsch had failed and this troublemaker, Hitler, was locked in jail. Germans agreed that these were bad, even desperate times, but they recoiled, disgusted, from rebels who would seize power with guns in their hands. Reported the New York *Times* to American readers: "The Munich putsch definitely eliminates Hitler and his National Socialist followers."

Three months after the bloodletting on the Munich street, Hitler and eight other defendants, including Ludendorff and Hess, were led into a courtroom to be tried on charges of treason against the government. The penalty could be death by hanging. "Only a miracle can save him," wrote Captain Truman Smith, an American officer assigned to the trial by the U.S. State Department. But, as Captain Smith reported, "a miracle happened."

8

"Hitler Is a Tiger!"

Hitler glared up at the black-robed judge, who had hurled down the question from the bench. "What right had you," the judge had asked, "to set yourself up as a dictator of Germany?"

The courtroom, packed with spectators and reporters, sat hushed, waiting for Hitler's reply. He brushed back the forelock of hair over his forehead, his pale face "all corners and angles," one reporter later wrote. He began to speak.

"A bird must sing because it is a bird!" he shouted. "A man who is born to be a dictator has a right to step forward and become a dictator."

Spectators burst into applause. Hitler smiled at the three judges. Only a few weeks before he had talked of killing himself. But now he was soaring toward one of his high moods. He had turned this courtroom, where he and his henchmen were being tried for treason, into a stage on which he was shouting his ideas and goals to an entranced Germany. "This man Hitler," people said all over the country, "says things that other politicians are afraid to say. Even if you disagree with him, you know he speaks what he believes."

After weeks of bombastic speeches Hitler concluded his defense, his searching eyes fixed on the judges: "For it is not you, gentlemen, who pass judgment on us. That judgment is spoken by the eternal court of history. What judgment you will hand down I know. But that [other] court will not ask us, 'Did you commit high treason or did you not?' That court will judge us . . . as Germans who wanted only the good of their people and their fatherland. . . . You may pronounce us guilty a thousand times over, but the goddess of the eternal court of history will smile and tear to tatters the brief of the state prosecutor and the sentence of this court. For she acquits us."

He sat down, and the spectators burst into applause. His fellow defendants—Hess, Ludendroff, and six others—clapped him on the back. He had turned this trial, as he later said, "into a sounding board" that echoed and reechoed his name and ideas around the world.

Hitler and seven other Nazis were found guilty (the old war hero, Ludendorff, was acquitted). Hitler could have been hanged or jailed for life. He was sentenced, instead, to five years. The judges knew he would be free within a year.

Thousands cheered him outside the courtroom. A smiling Hitler turned to Hess and said, "The republic won the battle, but we won the war."

In late April, 1924, Hitler was imprisoned in the fortresslike Landsberg Prison, nestled in the rolling green hills of Bavaria. He was given his own room. Thousands of letters and gifts poured into the prison from admirers; women flocked to Landsberg to glimpse him when he took his morning walk around the outside of the building.

One letter, from a young Berlin playwright, read: "To you, a god has given the tongue with which to express our sufferings." The young man signed his name: Joseph Paul Goebbels.

Stacked on tables in the small rooms were books by German philosophers. He read volumes of books by such writers as Nietzsche. Landsberg Prison, Hitler later said, "was my university at the state's expense."

He began to write a book about his life. He titled it "Four and a Half Years of Struggle Against Lies, Stupidities and Cowardice," but the publisher later shortened it to "My Struggle," in German, *Mein Kampf*. Within a few years the title would become among the most famous of all time.

Millions of copies of the book were sold in Germany and translated into dozens of languages. Yet only a few historians and scholars read the book from cover to cover. The words flew at the readers so thick and fast that they numbed the senses. "Reading the book," a critic said, "was like dragging one's feet through a mucky swamp."

When Hitler became famous, his followers bought the book, read a few pages, then placed it in a prominent place in their homes to show they were loyal Nazis. In other countries some critics called the book the meanderings of a madman. But if the world and Germany had paid closer attention to *Mein Kampf*, they would have read Hitler's blueprint for world conquest. "Whatever I did," he said later, "I promised I would do in *Mein Kampf*. If I had known I would become the ruler of Germany, I would never have written that book, because it told my enemies what to expect."

Fortunately for Hitler, France didn't believe *Mein Kampf* when he swore to destroy France, "the mortal enemy of the German people." Nor did the countries to the east of Germany believe him when he swore to gobble up those countries, as he marched toward Russia. Then he would conquer Russia, building an empire stretching from the Atlantic to the Pacific. Some 60,000,000 Germans, he promised, would be the masters of some 400,000,000 members of the "inferior races."

What right had Germany to enslave nearly half the world? In *Mein Kampf* he answered the question bluntly. "Who is at fault when the cat eats the mouse? One being drinks the blood of another. The stronger must dominate the weaker. . . . We should not blather about humanity. This was the iron law of nature."

This empire would be ruled by one man—himself. "There must be no majority decisions . . . the decisions will be made by one man . . . only he alone possesses the authority and the right to command."

Under him would be the German people, "the modern Aryans, thus the master race . . . the highest species of humanity on this earth." With confused and scientifically inaccurate explanations, Hitler sought to prove why the Germans were the master race. "The first culture arose with the Aryans. . . . In his encounters with lower people, the Aryan subjugated them and bent them to his will." Thus, concuded Hitler, the modern Aryan—the German—must bend other "lower people" to his will.

The enemy of the Aryan, he wrote, "was the Jewish people." Ignoring the evidence of the Bible, he claimed that "the Jew never had a culture of his own. . . . He is and remains the typical parasite." That parasite, he promised, would be destroyed.

Shortly before Christmas, 1924, after only nine months' imprisonment, the thirty-five-year-old Hitler walked out of Landsberg Prison. For at least two years, he was forbidden to speak in public. His Nazi party had been torn apart by fighting among his henchmen, infighting that he had stood by and watched. He knew that as long as his leaders were fighting among themselves, no one could rise to take his place as Nazi leader.

Hitler came out of jail to see a Germany rising to its feet after inflation had passed by like a summer rainstorm. A number of German financial wizards had steadied the mark, pegging it firmly so that it no longer soared upward by the hour. And during these Golden Twenties rich American investors began to pour money into German factories that were cranking out some of the finest products in the world: delicate cameras, high-powered sports cars, and other precisely engineered products. "If it is German-made," people in America said, "it is expensive, but it is good."

Once more happy Germans swarmed into bustling factories and offices. They were well paid. At night they ate and drank, pork and potatoes on the family table, steins of foaming beer on the tables of noisy beer halls. Germans now smirked when they talked about Hitler. No longer were they anxious for a "man on horseback" to shatter a peaceful and happy Germany. They laughed and turned their backs when Nazi speakers cried out against "scheming Jews" and "murdering Bolsheviks." By 1925 party membership had dwindled to only 700 members.

But Hitler decided to play a waiting game. One afternoon he said to a party leader, "Perhaps another twenty years or a hundred years may pass before our idea is victorious."

He was surrounded by a circle of tough aides. An even-fatter Goering had returned from Sweden, where he had fled after the putsch. Roehm sailed home from South America. And a twenty-eight-year-old poet and playwright joined the party and soon was nearly always at Hitler's side. He was Joseph Goebbels, a thin-faced, slender man no more than five feet tall; his foot had been deformed by a childhood bone disease, and he walked with a limp. Writing in his diary of his first meeting with Hitler, he described how Hitler had shaken his hand, "like an old friend. And those big blue eyes. Like stars. . . ."

Then there was the mushy-faced, nearsighted former clerk and chicken farmer, Heinrich Himmler, who had been part of a detachment of storm troopers during the putsch. Himmler organized a new private army. It was called the *Schutzstaffel,* or SS. The SS men wore black uniforms with a death's-head insignia and, as Hitler's private army, swore a secret oath to defend him against anyone, even the storm troopers, the police, or the army. The SS men were younger, stronger, and better trained than the paunchy "Old Fighters" who were storm troopers. Soon Roehm and his brownshirts were looking at Himmler's SS men with jealousy.

The beetle-browed, scowling Rudolf Hess, who had come out of Landsberg with Hitler, had become his secretary. But a blunt-faced former farmer with piglike eyes edged his way closer to Hitler as a secretary. He seemed able to read Hitler's mind and know exactly what he wanted. His name was Martin Bormann.

Hitler liked to see the people around him quarreling among themselves. He didn't want alliances formed that might become strong enough to topple him. And he wanted others to agree with him. "I do not look for people having clever ideas of their own," he once said, "but rather people who are clever in finding ways and means of carrying out my ideas."

"Absolutely no one could ever persuade him to change his mind once it was made up," a friend said. "On a number of occasions when his followers tried to talk him out of something, I noticed the faraway, unheeding expression in his eyes. It was as though he had closed his mind to all ideas but his own."

"I wait for an inner voice to guide me," he once whispered to Himmler confidentially. And to someone else he shouted, "Do you realize you are in the presence of the greatest German of all time —Adolf Hitler!"

But now the greatest German of all time had to play a waiting game. He traveled around the country, conferring with small groups of Nazis. As party leader he was paid a salary of about $100 a week. In Munich he lived in a small one-bedroom apartment. He also rented a small cottage south of Munich, high in the Bavarian Alps, overlooking the small town of Berchtesgaden. From his window he could look out and see the snowcapped peaks.

In Berchtesgaden he liked to be called Herr Wolf. Often, sitting in a small restaurant, he and his friends overheard Germans talking about "that madman Hitler." Hitler would smile, enjoying his masquerade.

He often attended the movies and the opera. His favorite movies were adventure thrillers. His favorite opera was Wagner's *Götterdämmerung*, and he was thrilled—no matter how often he saw it—by the final act as the temple of the gods collapsed amid flashes of lightning. When the thundering, tumultuous music filled the opera house, Hitler's knuckles whitened as he grasped the railings of his box seat.

He did not drink or smoke, considering both alcohol and tobacco "disgusting and immoral." But he retained his fondness for sweet, sticky pastries. Driving in his car, he would sometimes shout to his chauffeur to stop the car when they passed a pastry shop. He often stuffed down a chocolate-layer cake all by himself, seated in the back seat of the car, his eyes glazed over, seeming to have forgotten everything except the cake's deliciousness.

But such moments—when he showed that he was a real person with human tastes and emotion—were rare. More and more he seemed to try to portray himself as a stone-cold, unfeeling idol. He liked to play with scampering dogs, but if he saw that someone was watching him, he roughly chased the dogs away. He never appeared in public in a bathing suit, nor would he allow himself to be seen on a horse. He was afraid that he would be thrown from the horse and look ridiculous.

Occasionally he appeared in public with society women who had donated money to the party. And hundreds of women rushed to his side whenever he made a public appearance, throwing out their hands to touch him and begging, with inviting mouths, to be kissed. He walked coldly, eyes straight ahead, by them all.

"I could never marry," he once told a woman. "Imagine if on top of everything else I had a woman who interfered with my work! In my leisure time I want peace."

If he married, those wealthy women who gave money to the Nazis would lose interest in him, he said. Women who attended Nazi Party rallies might stop coming to them. "Lots of women are attracted to me because I am unmarried. It's the same as with a movie actor. When he marries, he loses a certain something for the women who adore him. Then he is no longer their idol as he was before."

In 1927, however, he seemed to have fallen in love. The girl was Geli Raubal, the daughter of his half sister, Angela. She was twenty, with long blond hair and twinkling blue eyes. Geli lived in Hitler's Berchtesgaden villa with her mother, who had become Hitler's housekeeper.

At first the sparkling Geli seemed fascinated by Hitler, even though he was almost twice her age. Party members began to hint that at last the Fuehrer would wed. Some, though, muttered that it was wrong for Hitler to marry a girl who was legally his niece.

After a year during which Hitler was seldom very far from Geli's side, they began to quarrel. She told him she wanted to go to Vienna, as he had twenty years before, "to be something" —in her case, an opera singer.

Hitler refused to let her leave him. Their quarrels became louder. Geli often cried and told her mother that she felt like a prisoner. And she hinted to friends that she was repelled by acts that Hilter wanted her to perform. Years of having denied himself the company of women may have warped Hitler, and some, close to him, believed he was unable to have a normal and healthy sexual relationship. "I love Geli, and I could marry her," he told a friend one day. But he would not marry her, he said, because he had to remain a bachelor. On the other hand, he wanted no one else to marry Geli.

In 1931 Hitler moved into a rambling nine-room apartment in Munich. Geli lived in one of the rooms. One morning, as Hitler walked out of the building and was about to step into his limousine, Geli called to him from an upstairs window, "Then you won't let me go to Vienna?"

"No!" he shouted. He jumped into the limousine and slammed the door.

That afternoon Geli, weeping, rode back to Hitler's cottage in Berchtesgaden. The next morning she was found dead in her room with a bullet in her heart.

She had apparently committed suicide. There were rumors that Hitler's SS men had murdered her to prevent an uncle-niece marriage that might have caused some Germans to resign from the party. But most historians believe she killed herself to escape Hitler.

Her death shook Hitler. For months he walked into party meetings with a dazed look on his face, his eyes glassy. But slowly he began to move out of his fog, for in 1931 he was reaching once more for the steering wheel of power.

The stock market crash of 1929 on Wall Street began to dry up the flood of American money into Germany. Then the worldwide depression shut down overseas demand for German products. German factories closed their doors. The lines of unemployed increased from 3,000,000 in 1929 to almost 6,000,000 by 1932.

Once more Hitler stood on platforms promising to cure German misery. Hungry men began to pour into the barracks of the storm troopers for free soup and a roof over their heads. By 1932 the storm troopers numbered as many men as the German army, which was limited by the Treaty of Versailles to 100,000. Once more the storm troopers swaggered through German streets. With clubs and pistols, they battled Communists in the streets. They smashed their way into the meetings of Communists. "The storm troopers," said one Nazi, "have become the battering ram of the party."

Crisscrossing the country, Hitler spoke to thousands of meetings of people who were frightened and shocked by the sudden fall from good times to poverty. At meeting after meeting, accompanied by the entrance music of the "Badenweiler March," he strode down an aisle to the platform, spotlights playing on him. People rose and threw out their arms in the Nazi salute, shouting for Hitler and for victory: "Heil Hitler! Sieg Heil! Heil Hitler! Sieg Heil!"

Hitler, pounding a fist on the podium, told them what had gone wrong. He blamed the rich. He blamed the Communists. He blamed the Jews. He blamed everyone. Only one man, he shouted, his metallic voice almost hysterical as he swayed on the platform, his fists clenched, could "bring back the good old days. . . ." That man was himself. At the end the crowds surged toward him, the chant becoming a frenzy: "Hail Hitler, Hail Victory, Hail Hitler, Hail Victory!"

In the elections of 1930, the Nazis won 107 seats in the Reichstag (the German legislature)—almost one of every five. Their total vote was more than 6,500,000. From being the ninth-place party in the Reichstag, the Nazis had jumped to second. A confident Hitler told Goebbels, "The victory of our movement will take place at the most in two and a half to three years."

A year later the 1933 presidential election was approaching. The President was the eighty-five-year-old Paul von Hindenburg, a former general and war hero, who was looked upon as a wise grandfather by most Germans. Goebbels, Goering, and other Nazis tried to tempt Hitler to run against Hindenburg for the presidency.

Hitler hesitated. "We are rolling along on a wave of invincibility," he told Goebbels and Goering one afternoon as they sat at a table in Nazi Party headquarters in Berlin. "If we run against Hindenburg and lose, we may no longer seem to the masses as being on the way up and impossible to stop."

"It's a risk," Goebbels conceded, "but it must be taken." If Hindenburg became President for another seven-year term, Goebbels argued, he might put through laws that would outlaw both the Nazi and Communist parties as a way to block their bloody battling in the streets.

For the next few weeks Hitler brooded over what he should do. Other Nazis pleaded with Goebbels and Goering to convince Hitler to run. "We fear the Fuehrer is waiting too long," the leaders pleaded. "If he waits any longer, people will think he is too weak and indecisive to be a President."

On the night of February 22, 1933, Goebbels met with Hitler in a hotel room across the street from the President's palace. Again Goebbels tried to talk Hitler into running. Hitler put up his hand. "I have made my decision," he said. "You will announce it tonight."

That night a smiling Goebbels stood on the speakers' platform before a packed meeting of Nazis in the Berlin sports palace. Spotlights swung circles of light around the dwarfish Nazi propaganda chief as he raised his hand to silence the audience. He had an important message to read to them—directly from the Fuehrer.

The hall grew hushed. Goebbels threw up both hands as he

shouted, in his squeaky voice, "The Fuehrer will run against Hindenburg for the presidency!"

The Nazis stood and roared. Across the street, in the hotel room, Hitler talked to a Nazi lawyer, Hans Frank. Hitler had plunged into one of his depressed moods. "I know," he said gloomily, "that I never will be President."

He was right—but soon he would be more than President.

9

"Your Death Knell Has Sounded"

Hitler paced the floor of the hotel room. Watching him worriedly were his three chief lieutenants: the scar-faced Roehm, the fat Goering, and the gnomish Goebbels. Hitler stopped pacing, turned, and glared at them as they sat around a circular wooden table. "If the party ever falls apart," Hitler said, his hollow voice reverberating dramatically, "it won't take me more than three minutes to kill myself."

The time was the autumn of 1932. That spring he had run against Hindenburg for the presidency of the republic and lost, 19,300,000 votes to 13,400,000. But Hitler had pulled in more votes than he had expected. "Hindenburg is eighty-five," Hitler had told Goebbels. "I am forty-five. I can wait."

But by November, 1932, six months later, he was worried. In a July election for the Reichstag, the Nazis had won 230 seats. They then possessed more votes in the Reichstag—the lawmaking "Congress" of the republic—than any other party. But in November, when another election was held, the number of Nazi seats dropped to 196.

Three election campaigns in six months had drained the party treasury. Standing on the street corners of German towns, Nazi storm troopers rattled tin cups and begged for contributions for "the wicked old Nazis." Other brownshirts—the brawling street fighters of the past ten years—grumbled loudly over their steins of beer, arguing that the Nazis should march into Hindenburg's palace in Berlin and throw the "old Prussian" out into the street. Hitler feared that his roughnecks would indeed march on Berlin in another putsch. It would fail, he knew, and it would give Hindenburg an excuse to jail Hitler and outlaw the Nazi Party.

Worried now that he had failed, he talked in the hotel room of suicide. But during the next few hours Goering, Goebbels, and Roehm convinced him that he should try to outmaneuver Hindenburg and his other rivals to grab the reins of power. "The chess game for power has begun," Goebbels wrote delightedly in his diary.

The Nazis faced four principal rivals. One was the rich and titled landowners of Prussia, the aristocratic "vons" like Hindenburg. A second rival for power was the rich industrialists of Germany's Ruhr, the "smokestack" region of Germany dotted with factories. A third rival was the army's generals. The fourth was the Communist Party and its factory and railroad workers, millions strong, who could brake the country to a paralyzing stop by walking off their jobs whenever their Communist leaders called for a general strike.

Hitler's brownshirts battled the Communist workers in the streets. In one year more than 4,000 Nazis and Communists were injured and more than 100 killed in these club-swinging battles.

By that time there were more than 500,000 storm troopers, five times the size of the German army. In addition, Hitler could call on his private army of black-shirted, pistol-carrying SS men, and

Goering had organized a Nazi police force. It was called the *Geheime Staatspolizei* (secret state police) and soon became known—and dreaded—as the Gestapo. It numbered more than 50,000 men, who had spies in every factory and office, and in many homes as well. A German who dared to talk against Hitler might be awakened at night by a knocking on the door. He would be dragged from his home by storm troopers, SS men, or Gestapo, beaten, and perhaps even killed. "Germany is a territory occupied by Hitler's private armies," said one German general sourly in 1932.

Emboldened by their growing strength, five SS men swarmed into the home of a Communist leader in Silesia, a state in eastern Germany. They dragged him from his bed and, while his mother watched in horror, trampled him to death.

The SS men were arrested by the police, tried in court, found guilty, and sentenced to death. Hitler protested angrily and promised, in a telegram to the murderers, "to save them from this monstrous bloodthirsty sentence." He slammed into the office of Germany's Vice-Chancellor, the number two post in the government, and told Vice-Chancellor Franz von Papen that he would unleash his brownshirts if the five weren't immediately released. The brownshirts, he swore, "would roar through the streets and tear enemies limb from limb."

Fearing a civil war, President Hindenburg commuted the sentences to life imprisonment. A few months later the SS men walked, laughing, out of jail. A grinning Hitler told the commanders of his SS and brownshirt armies, "We must have the capacity to commit cruelties with a clear conscience."

In late 1932 and early 1933 Hitler went on playing the chess game for power. He marched his private armies through the streets of German cities to impress Hindenburg, his Prussian friends, the generals, and the industrialists with the strength that stood behind him. He appealed to the real fear of conservatives: that the Communists would seize the country and its wealth. Luridly he described how "the Communist butchers" would slaughter the rich in their beds, hang the generals, and enslave the population. Only he, Adolf Hitler, with his powerful armies, could stop the Communists and wipe them out.

The Nazis demanded that President Hindenburg appoint Hitler as Chancellor. "Never," said the crusty old war hero. "I might appoint that Austrian corporal to run the post office, but never, never Chancellor."

But Hindenburg's son, fearful that the Communists might strip him of the family's vast estates, counseled his father to make Hitler the Chancellor. So did Papen and a number of generals and industrialists. "He will stop the Communists from taking over," they told the old President, who yearned for a peaceful Germany after some twenty years of world war and internal strife. "Once we have used Hitler to stamp out the Communists, we can topple him and get rid of him."

Hitler's opponents hadn't yet learned that you might ride on Hitler toward a goal. But when he threw you off, he would eat you. "He isn't a horse," a foe once said. "Hitler is a tiger."

On the morning of January 30, 1933, Hindenburg appointed Hitler the Chancellor of Germany, second in power only to the President. That night long columns of celebrating Nazi storm troopers marched through the streets of Berlin, carrying torches. "It was like a river of fire," said one viewer of that triumphal procession. After the long, cold, hungry years of fighting in the streets, Hilter's Old Fighters, as the storm troopers called them-selves, thought they were at the doorway of success—good jobs, power, and all of Germany's wealth, sitting there for them to snatch up.

Standing in the window of the presidential palace, Hitler

watched the long rivers of fire flow by, the endless columns shouting, "Heil Hitler!" and singing "Germany over All." By now there were 13,000,000 Germans enrolled in the Nazi Party, 1 of every 5 persons in the nation. "We need only to establish ourselves in office," the crafty Goebbels told Hitler, "and we will only leave when they carry us out dead."

Hitler, Goering, and Goebbels began to dig themselves into bases of power. Goering was elected head of the Reichstag. Goebbels became director of the Bureau of Propaganda. "Adolf Hitler is Germany, and Germany is Adolf Hitler," Rudolf Hess told millions of listeners on a government radio network that was now controlled by the Nazis. "He who pledges himself to Hitler pledges himself to Germany." "Hitler is never wrong," roared Goebbels.

Hitler and Goebbels began to plan for the Reichstag elections of March 5, 1933. "Now it will be easy to carry on the fight for Reichstag seats," Goebbels rejoiced in his diary. "Now we can call on the resources of the state. We can use the government radio network. And this time . . . there will be no shortage of money."

But Hitler was hoping for another boost to shove him toward the pinnacle of power. He thought that boost would come from—of all people—the Communists. He hoped they would pour workers into the streets to revolt against the new Chancellor. His Nazi storm troopers, armed with weapons and ammunition, would blow the workers off the streets with cannon shells and machine-gun fire. Then Hitler could stand in front of the German people and say, "See, I saved you from communism. I am the man who must be your leader."

The Communists sensed what Hitler wanted them to do. Their leaders hid in cellars and forests, biding their time. They believed that the industrialists and the generals would come to see that

Hitler, if he got the chance, would destroy them. "They'll eat up Hitler," said the Communists, "before he eats up them."

Hitler fretted as the Reichstag elections came closer. Why didn't the Communists strike?

"Now I have them!" Hitler shouted.

His eyes glistened with delight as Goebbels, having just put down the telephone in his apartment in Berlin, told him the news: The Reichstag building was aflame. Already the word was being spread through Berlin: The Communists had set it afire—their signal for a bloody revolution.

Hitler and Goebbels ran down the stairs of the apartment building and leaped into Hitler's black Mercedes. A chauffeur drove the car through the dark streets at more than 60 miles an hour. His head out the window of the car, Hitler could see the orange tongues of flame licking at the roof of the historic old building. "It is a sign from heaven," he shouted to Goebbels.

The car screeched to a stop amid the swirling red beacons of fire trucks. Hitler jumped out of the car and leaped over firemen's hoses as he ran into the lobby. Firemen were yanking the hoses up the staircase to pour water onto the fire in the cavernous chamber.

An ovenlike heat radiated from the fire inside the chamber. Hilter's face glowed red, partly from the heat and partly from the excitement. Reporters and officials gathered around him. "This is the beginning of the Communist uprising," he shrieked. "Now they are going to strike; not a minute must be lost."

He seemed to have lost control of himself. The words tumbled out in furious bursts. "Now there can be no mercy. Whoever gets in our way will be cut down. The German people will not put up with leniency. Every Communist functionary will be shot wherever we find him. The Communist deputies of the Reichstag may be hanged this very night. Everyone in alliance with the Communists will be arrested."

Minutes after arriving at the fire the police had arrested a suspect. He was a twenty-four-year-old Dutch tramp named Marinus Van der Lubbe, who had once been a member of the Communist Party. He loudly confessed to detectives that he had set fire to the building. Some of the detectives, who had arrested other pyromaniacs, wondered how this one man could have created this huge conflagration all by himself.

By dawn the police had obeyed the orders of Chancellor Hitler and arrested the leader of the Communists in the Reichstag and three other Communists. They were accused of having conspired with Van der Lubbe to burn the Reichstag.

All during the night and into the next day Germans tensed, waiting for the Communists to strike in other cities. Nothing happened. The suspicion began to grow: Had the fire been started by someone who wanted the Communists to be blamed?

Hitler acted quickly before those suspicions could spread too far. The morning after the fire he handed an "emergency decree" to President Hindenburg and urged him to sign it immediately. The decree gave Chancellor Hitler the power to arrest any person and search any house. It gave him the power to arrest any public speaker "beyond the legal limits of the Constitution."

Hitler wanted to place himself above the law. In short, he would be the law.

Reading the emergency decree, the aged Hindenburg shook his head. He knew that the decree would make Hitler even more powerful than the President and the Reichstag. At first he growled that he would not sign. Calmly, Hitler assured him that the decree would be only temporary. Hitler reminded the President that the Communists might set aflame the fields of Hindenburg's estates in Prussia. Still mumbling to himself, Hindenburg signed the decree.

During the next few days Roehm's storm troopers, Heinrich Himmler's SS gunmen, and Goering's Gestapo arrested, beat, tortured, and killed Communists. More than 4,000 men and women were thrown into concentration camps. "If resistance is offered," Goebbels told the Nazis in a radio address, "then clear the streets." And Goering told his brutal Gestapo police, "I don't have to worry about justice. My mission is only to exterminate and destroy."

There was no surge by the Communists into the streets to take over the government. Hitler and the Nazis took credit for quashing the revolt before it could begin.

A few weeks after the fire the trial of Van der Lubbe and the four Communist leaders began. As leader of the Reichstag the bejowled Goering testified he had reason to think the Communist leaders conspired to burn the building as a flaming signal to begin their revolution. But the Communist leaders could prove that they were not near the Reichstag when the fire began. And after staring at the sickly, drooling Van der Lubbe, who was obviously demented, one reporter wrote: "It was impossible to believe that this weak young man could have set that huge fire all by himself."

At the end of the trial Goering glared as the judges found the four Communist leaders innocent. They did find Van der Lubbe guilty, and he was sentenced to death. A few days later he walked to a scaffold, where he would be beheaded. Just as he was about to climb the steps to the scaffold, the young man began to scream. Years later witnesses swore that his last words were: "Not alone ... not alone. . . ."

No one has ever been able to prove or disprove what many in Germany believed at the time: that the Nazis themselves set the fire to pin the blame on the Communists and pave the way for Hitler to destroy his enemies. But there is no doubt that the

Reichstag fire did frighten millions of German voters. The night of the fire German farmers grabbed shotguns and stood guard all night over their land, peering into the darkness for the torches of marauding Communist workers. On the radio Goebbels' propagandists screamed all during the night that "the Bolshevist butchers are on the march!" With many Germans still fearful of a bloody Red revolution, voters walked to polling places on March 5, 1933, a week after the fire. Some 17,000,000 voted for Nazi candidates for the Reichstag. They elected 288 Nazis, almost half the total number in the Reichstag.

Hitler immediately began to scheme for more power. He wanted the Reichstag to pass a law called the Enabling Act. If the Enabling Act were passed, Hitler would transcend—not temporarily, but permanently—both the Reichstag and the presidency. As Chancellor he would be Germany's ruler.

To pass the Enabling Act, he needed the vote of two of every three deputies seated in the Reichstag. He could count on the votes of only one of every two—about 53 percent to be exact. He needed 67 percent.

Goering sat down with Hitler and, grinning, told him how Hitler could get two of every three votes in the Reichstag. "We will arrest all the Communist deputies in the Reichstag," he said, laughing; "under some pretext or other. Then we will arrest a few other deputies. Of those that are left, most will be Nazis, and you will easily get sixty-seven percent of the votes."

The day of the vote storm troopers paraded around the Reichstag building, where the deputies were meeting in the still-blackened chamber. The storm troopers chanted, "Full power or else . . . full power or else. . ."

A few brave Germans rose in the Reichstag chamber to speak out against the Enabling Act that would put a bullet to the head of the republic. An angry Hitler leaped to his feet and interrupted one of the speakers. "You are no longer needed," he snarled at the startled anti-Nazi. "Your death knell has sounded."

Minutes later the vote was taken. The Enabling Act was passed by far better than a two-thirds vote, the tally: 441 for, only 84 against. As the vote was announced, the Nazi deputies stood and cheered, while outside the storm troopers sang "Raise High the Flag" and chanted, "Heil Hitler! Heil Hitler!"

The German democracy had been smashed into bits by Hitler's sledgehammer blows. In its place stood what Hitler called the Third Reich. The First Reich had been the Holy Roman Empire that Charlemagne had begun in 800 and that had lasted in central Europe until 1806. The Second Reich had been the powerful Germany built by Otto von Bismarck, the wily Prussian who had cemented together the German states into the most powerful nation of Europe from 1871 to 1918. His Third Reich, Hitler proclaimed, would last 1,000 years. Proudly he told the cheering Nazi deputies, "We are the last who will be making history in Germany!"

Armed with the powers of the Enabling Act, Hitler moved swiftly to take over the country. Labor unions were crushed, their leaders killed, beaten, or imprisoned. The Nazi Party booted factory owners out of their offices, especially if they were Jews, and took command of huge factories. "What a fool I was," growled Ruhr magnate Fritz Thyssen, "to have supported Hitler."

Governors of German states were dismissed from office and replaced by loyal Nazis. Anti-Nazi books were burned in the streets by storm troopers, more than 20,000 copies of "un-German writing" vanishing amid smoke and flames in the public squares of cities. Newspaper and magazine editors were told they could print only "news" fed to them by Goebbels' propaganda writers. All news from the outside world had to pass through Goebbels' censors. They screened out news that the Nazis didn't want Germans to read. Radio stations could broadcast only music and news approved by Goebbels. Germans could see only movies—made in America or in Germany—that were first approved by Hitler. Hitler was capturing both the bodies and the minds of Germans.

The windows of Jewish shops were shattered by storm troopers while police stood by helplessly, knowing that if an arrest were made, the storm trooper would be freed by Nazi judges. "Hitler," crowed Goering, "is the law!"

"The government will strike down with all brutality anyone who opposes it," warned the Nazi leader in the state of Württemberg. "We do not say an eye for an eye and a tooth for a tooth. No, if anyone strikes an eye from us, we will chop off his head. And if anyone knocks out one of our teeth, we will smash in his jaw."

Some German conservatives came to Hitler's office to complain of the storm troopers' "rowdyism and murder in the streets." Hitler stood up and ordered them to leave. "No longer bring me your complaints," he snarled. "History will say that the Nazis— in this historic hour—acted to exterminate Marxism with kid gloves instead of the iron fist."

But during the first few months of what Hitler called "a National Rising," 'the Nazis murdered an estimated 500 to 600 political opponents. About 100,000 others—Communists, conservatives, Jews, and other "enemies of the state"—were now staring with frightened eyes from behind the barbed wire of concentration camps. From places like Dachau a few Germans returned, their heads shaved, their faces gaunt, their eyes frightened, to whisper to a few friends of beatings, tortures, executions.

Seated in his office in the ornate Chancellery, lounging behind the desk once used by the revered Bismarck—"the George Washington of Germany"—Hitler gloated to cronies like Goering and Goebbels, "Who would have thought the takeover would have been so easy?" And speaking of the remnants of the opposition—

the shocked generals and Prussians—he said darkly, "They are going to set traps for me. But we will not wait until they act. We are ruthless. I have no scruples. . . . The conservatives think I am uncultured, a barbarian. Yes, we are barbarians. . . . We are the ones who will remake the world. The old world is done for!"

During the National Rising, Hitler's Old Fighters—the brown-shirted storm troopers who had fought with bare knuckles, clubs, and guns during the past ten years to clear the streets for Hitler —now talked eagerly of how they would be rewarded with riches. Most were unemployed. They wanted jobs—high-paying jobs in city halls, banks, the offices of factories. They wanted to be the mayors, company presidents, city officials, the high-paid executives and bosses of the new Germany. Hungry, bitter, and out of work for years, they expected to pocket the riches of victory.

But there were millions of Old Fighters and there were only a few thousand of those cushy, high-paying jobs. Most of the Old Fighters watched as a few lucky ones sat behind desks, puffing cigars and getting fat on high salaries. Standing on street corners, hungry and still wearing the dirty uniforms of their street-fighting days, the storm troopers began to grumble. Their leader, the tough Ernst Roehm, was also grumbling. Hitler, he told his aides, had forgotten his army.

Roehm began to shout for "a second revolution." He talked with his generals of a Night of the Long Knives during which the storm troopers would slash the throats of the rich and take away their wealth with bloody hands.

Hitler wanted no "second revolution." The waves of another revolution could overwhelm him and his Nazis and sweep them out of office. But there would be a Night of the Long Knives— and soon. The knives would be thrust at the throats of Roehm and his storm troopers.

10

"I Know How to Do Justice"

The silvery three-engine Junker airplane droned through the darkness. Hitler sat next to the pilot in the front cabin. He was wearing a dark-brown leather jacket, brown shirt, black bow tie, and high black army boots. He stared through the windshield into the darkness. His face was pale and unshaved, the flesh around his eyes red and puffy because of lack of sleep. Looking to his left, Hitler could see a rosy line spreading along the horizon. Dawn was about to spill its white light onto Germany on this Saturday morning, June 30, 1934, as Hitler flew south on a mission of murder.

His target was Ernst Roehm, that scar-faced adventurer who had built the brown-shirted storm troopers into an army of 3,000,000 men. In caves, forests, and old buildings all over Germany the storm troopers had stored rifles, cannon, machine guns, bombs, and hand grenades. At any moment, on a signal from Roehm, the storm troopers were ready to put on their helmets, grab their guns, and begin what Roehm had been impatiently calling for—the second revolution.

Hitler had begged Roehm to be patient. High-paying jobs, he had promised, would be distributed to the Old Fighters during the early years of his regime.

But Roehm was impetuous. "Since I am a bad man," he once growled, "war appeals to me more than peace." And more than once he had bellowed to his storm troopers: "Hitler has turned his back against us. He is lining up with the old crowd that's always been running things—the generals, the Prussians, the bankers. We've got to root them out of office."

Roehm's warlike public speeches had alarmed everyone— Hitler and his Nazis as well as Hindenburg and his conservatives. Especially alarmed were Goering, Goebbels, and Himmler. They feared that if Roehm's second revolution succeeded, he would arrest them and make himself Hitler's number two man.

In Berlin during the past few months Goering, Goebbels, and Himmler had conspired against Roehm. They showed letters to Hitler that they had forged. The letters, Hitler said later, indicated to him that Roehm "was making preparations to eliminate me personally." The three plotters also showed faked documents to Hitler, so-called plans of the storm troopers to begin their second revolution late in June. On the night of June 29, as Hitler rested at a hotel on the Rhine near Cologne, the plotters sent to him a document indicating that the storm troopers were massing to march on Berlin and Munich.

Sweat glistened on Hitler's face as he read the document and then debated with Goebbels, who was with him, what to do. Perhaps he knew the document was faked, concocted by the conspirators. But now he had an excuse to quell his Old Fighters before they became so troublesome that Hindenburg would have to declare martial law. There could be fighting between his Old Fighters and the army, fighting that would cost Chancellor Hitler heavily in prestige in Germany and around the world. And if the Old Fighters won, they might in their anger throw Hitler out of office or even kill him. As much as he dreaded turning against his old comrades, Hitler knew he had to act.

His face chalky white, Hitler left the hotel. He jumped into a Mercedes and drove quickly to an airport, the time near midnight. He clambered aboard his private Junker, which now flew through the night toward Roehm and his storm troopers in Munich.

There, instead of assembling for a bloody revolution, Roehm and his lieutenants had been drinking beer and carousing much of the night at a hotel about an hour's drive from Munich. Now they were snoring blissfully, unaware that danger winged closer by the minute.

Roehm had only talked of a second revolution. There had been no serious planning. Almost doglike in his devotion to Hitler, Roehm had been heartsick when he thought the Fuehrer had turned his back on the Old Fighters. But within the past week his spirits had soared. Hitler had phoned him! He had told Roehm to call his chief commanders and order them to report to Munich on the weekend of June 30. Hitler would fly to Munich to address the storm trooper leaders. "Adolf has come over to our side of things," an excited Roehm told his commanders. "He will march with us, I am sure of it, when the revolution begins."

Hitler's plane set down on a runway of the Munich airport shortly after four in the morning of June 30. As Hitler stepped from the plane into the gray early-morning light, he saw armored cars and truckloads of helmeted troops massed around the airport. In Berlin Goering had ordered army units to roll into Munich to stop what he was reporting as an uprising by the brownshirts.

Hilter's face twitched as he walked toward a black limousine. "This is the hardest, the worst day of my life," Hitler said to an army officer who walked with him. "But, believe me, I know how to do justice."

Behind the car was stretched a long line of cars and trucks. They were filled with black-uniformed SS men, pistols crammed into their pockets. Hitler and Goebbels slipped into the rear seat of the limousine. "To the Ministry of the Interior," Hitler ordered the driver. The Ministry of the Interior was the headquarters of the brownshirts.

At the ministry Hitler leaped out of the car, gripping a revolver in his right hand. The other cars screeched to a stop behind Hitler's. Dozens of SS men followed Hitler as he swept through the front door.

A brown-shirted storm trooper officer, seated behind a table in the hallway, rose in astonishment as he saw Hitler's famous face, which was contorted with rage. The officer rose and began to extend his arm in the Nazi salute. "Heil—"

Hitler rushed at him, arms wide as though ready to choke him. "Lock him up!" he shrieked. An SS man grabbed the storm trooper and dragged him through the front door and down the steps, then hurled him into a car.

Other storm troopers ran into the hallway, many in their pajamas, having been awakened by the shouts and noise. "They are traitors, your leaders are traitors!" Hitler screamed.

Minutes later the leader of the storm troopers in Bavaria arrived. "You are under arrest, traitor!" Hitler snapped, aiming the pistol at the startled commander's face. "You will be shot!" The stunned commander was pulled, screaming, out of the room and sped to a nearby prison. There, during the next few hours, the prison courtyard filled with storm trooper leaders, each asking others, "What is this all about? Do you know anything?"

By eight in the morning Hitler's car was streaking toward the lakeside resort of Bad Weissee, leading a caravan of cars filled with SS men. They were headed toward the hotel where Roehm, with his aides, still slept.

At the hotel Hitler jumped out of the car, flanked by two SS men. He was still carrying a pistol. An SS man kicked in the locked front door, and Hitler strode into the hotel's hallway.

A maid, coming out of a room, gaped as she saw the Nazi Fuehrer. Other storm troopers, hearing the pounding of heavy boots in the hall, opened bedroom doors. They stared at the wild-eyed, pistol-waving Hitler.

"Arrest them!" Hitler ordered. SS men grabbed the startled storm troopers, most still in pajamas, and punched, shoved, and kicked them down the hallway.

"I haven't done anything!" a storm trooper pleaded with an SS man he knew. "Help me!"

"I can do nothing," the SS man growled.

The storm troopers were herded downstairs and into the cellar, a door locked behind them.

Hitler and an SS man banged on the door of Roehm's room. Blinking, Roehm raised himself on his bed and said, groggily, "Who's there?"

"An SS officer."

Roehm got up and opened the door. His heavy-lidded eyes stared unbelievingly at Hitler's face.

"Heil, my Fuehrer!" he stuttered, beginning to raise his arm.

Hitler lunged at him, shoving him backward. "You are under arrest!"

Roehm began to ask why. Hitler spun and stalked out of the room. The SS man led Roehm to the cellar.

Minutes later the prisoners were marched out of the cellar and pushed into cars. They were taken to the prison courtyard in Munich. Hitler followed in his car. In Munich he drove to the railroad station. He stood in a dark corner, watching as dozens of storm troopers began to arrive on trains from all over Germany for the weekend conference called by Roehm. The storm troopers swaggered down the station platform in their heavy boots, laughing and clapping each other on the shoulders, talking excitedly about what they expected to hear from the Fuehrer when he addressed them.

Moments later, as they reached the end of the platform, they felt guns stuck into their ribs and heard the harsh orders of SS men telling them to do as they were told—quickly. They were hurled into cars, those who protested slugged and knocked unconscious. Within minutes they joined almost 200 other Old Fighters who now cowered in the prison courtyard, the afternoon sunlight warming their shocked and frightened faces.

At the Brown House, a storm trooper headquarters in Munich, Goebbels had been busy scribbling down names on long sheets of paper. He was writing out lists of storm troopers and others —to be murdered. Then he picked up a phone and called Goering in Berlin. When Goering came onto the line and identified himself, Goebbels said only one word, *"Kolibri,"* then hung up.

Kolibri was the German word for hummingbird. It was the signal that Roehm had been seized and that it was time for the killings to begin.

During the day, in Berlin, lists had been drawn up by Goering and Himmler. The lists were the names of the storm trooper leaders most loyal to Roehm. But Goebbels, Goering, and Himmler had taken advantage of what they called "this unique opportunity" to slaughter others who had stood in their way or in Hitler's way in the climb to power.

Names on the lists were jotted down on short slips of paper, two or three names on each slip. The slips were placed in envelopes stamped with a swastika seal. The envelopes were handed out to SS gunmen, who raced off in cars to hunt down their victims.

Gregor Strasser had been a Hitler lieutenant in the party until only recently, when he had balked at one of the Fuehrer's orders and quit. He was dragged from his home and thrown into a room in the cellar of Gestapo headquarters in Berlin. From the shadows a gun was aimed at his head and fired three times. Strassser died in a pool of his own blood.

A Catholic party leader sat at his desk in Berlin when an SS man threw open the door and shouted he was under arrest. The Catholic leader rose, his eyes staring as he saw the SS man jerk out a gun. The gun bucked once, then twice, and the leader dropped, blood spurting from holes in his chest. The SS man walked to the desk, the leader draped over it. He picked up the phone and phoned SS headquarters. He said a few words, listened, then hung up. He placed the smoking gun in the dead man's hands, then walked out the door, where he and another SS man stood guard. To office workers who had come running at the sound of the shots, they said coldly, "Herr Direktor has killed himself."

A former Chancellor of Germany, General Kurt von Schleicher, was talking on the telephone in his home when the doorbell rang. A servant opened the door and saw five men in black raincoats, hands in their pockets.

They brushed by her, walked into the living room, and saw the general. "Are you General Schleicher?" one asked.

"Yes, I am General Schleicher," he said, turning toward them, phone still in his hand.

Two of the men pulled out guns that spit fire. Bullets ripped into the general, who crashed to the floor. His wife ran into the room. Again the guns roared, and she fell dead across her husband's body.

All that Saturday afternoon, Saturday evening, and on into

Sunday and Monday the guns of the SS tore open the bodies of men and women on the Nazi lists. They were gunned down in their homes and offices, blasted in alleys and streets, hunted like animals in forests and on dark country lanes.

Old scores were settled by Hitler. In Bavaria three men knocked at the door of Gustav von Kahr, the former Commissar of Bavaria who had sneaked away from Hitler's putsch. They threw Kahr into a car and sped away. Three days later his butchered body was found in a ditch, arms and body ripped by an ax.

Hitler's memory went even farther back. In a small German village a middle-aged man turned a corner, and his head was blown apart by a pistol bullet. Several hours later his bloody body was identified. He was Reinhold Hanisch, a former flophouse bum whose fatal mistake had been having known another flophouse bum named Adolf Hitler. As Al Capone's gangsters were saying while they gunned down rival gangsters in Chicago at the same time, "Dead men tell no tales."

In Munich that Saturday evening Hitler arrived at the Brown House from the railroad station. Goebbels handed him a list of the storm trooper leaders now captive inside the prison courtyard. Hitler began to mark X's next to some of the names. Watching at Hitler's side, Goebbels frowned when he saw Hitler's pen stop at Roehm's name, then move on without putting an X next to it. Roehm, Goebbels knew, had to die or his life and those of Goering and Himmler would never be safe from his vengeance.

Hitler handed the list to an SS officer. "Take six men with you and have these executed for high treason."

A half hour later, the shadows of the June evening darkening in the courtyard, the names of six storm troopers were called out. They rose warily, their seated comrades seeing the tear in their ashen faces. SS men led the six out of the courtyard, through a building, their boots clacking on the stone floor, and into another courtyard.

One of the six storm troopers was ordered to stand against a wall, facing the glass windows of the prison. The fading light glinted against the windows as an SS officer shouted, "By order of the Fuehrer, you are to be executed." He turned to the five SS men who faced the condemned man, rifles aimed at his quivering body. "Ready! Aim! Fire!"

Five rifles boomed. The storm trooper's body spun and collapsed to the ground. The SS officer walked over to it, aimed a pistol at the head and fired, the *coup de grâce* that grants sudden death for those not already dead.

The next storm trooper was marched to the wall. "This is madness!" he shouted. "We are innocent!"

"You have been condemned to death by the Fuehrer for high treason. Heil Hitler!"

Again the rifles cracked. In the nearby courtyard the other storm troopers stared at each other, silent, as burst after burst of gunfire echoed and reechoed against the stone walls.

Minutes later the SS men arrived at the Brown House and reported to Hitler. "The traitors have paid," the SS leader shouted, flashing out his right arm. "Heil Hitler!"

Hitler, face matted with beard and gaunt after more than thirty hours on his feet, walked to a room where other storm troopers had been herded. He stood before them.

"Your leadership has betrayed your confidence," he snapped. "It is now necessary to know whether you are with me or with those who deceived you. . . ."

A storm trooper jumped from his chair and shouted, "Heil Hitler!" Others stood, and soon each man was shouting over and over, "Heil Hitler!" with arms extended toward the glowering Hitler.

"You will go directly and separately to your homes," Hitler ordered. "There remove your uniforms. You will await orders that the storm troopers have been reorganized."

The Old Fighters walked out of the Brown House like whipped dogs under the sneering gazes of the SS men.

Late that afternoon Hitler flew back to Berlin, his Junker setting down at Tempelhof Airport against the background, appropriately enough, of a blood-red sky. Alighting from the plane, he was handed a list of those who had been killed so far. He silently began to check off the names of others to be killed. But once more his pen passed over the name of Roehm. Goebbels and Goering glanced at each other.

The next morning, July 1, Germans awoke on a sunny Sunday to read in the newspapers that Hitler personally had stamped out "the second revolution by the storm troopers." With words fed to them by Goebbels' propaganda writers, the newspapers reported that "the government has struck with staggering accuracy and has done all it could to assure the tranquillity of every patriot, who no longer need fear any harm or disturbance. . . . We now have a strong, consolidated, and purified state."

Berlin, on that sunny summer afternoon, appeared calm as children frolicked in the city parks and families walked and biked, picnic baskets in hand, to the lakes and forests that ringed the city.

But at a military school on the outskirts of Berlin rifle fire crackled all morning and on into the afternoon. More than 150 top brownshirt leaders, brought there from all over Germany, had been kept all night in a coal cellar. The next day they were led out, four at a time, marched to a wall in a courtyard. An SS man ripped open their shirts and marked a black circle, with charcoal, on their chests. Then an officer stepped back, shouted,

"The Fuehrer wills it! Heil Hitler! Fire!" And the eight rifles of a firing squad drilled bullets into the chests of the doomed brown-shirts, some of whom shouted, "Heil Hitler!" moments before the firing began. Most could not believe that their beloved Hitler had marked them to die. People around the military school jammed hands over ears to shut out the nerve-tearing din of the rifle fire. They watched butcher trucks pull up to the school and then roll away, trailing streams of blood.

That Sunday afternoon Hitler walked among guests at a party at his Chancellery, tousling the heads of Goebbels' children, who ran giggling from table to table, snatching sweets and cups of soft drinks. A band played the "Badenweiler March," as Hitler smiled and shook hands with the guests, many of them the families of foreign diplomats.

Hitler was called to a room by Goebbels and Goering. They told him that army generals were enraged by the murder of their fellow general Schleicher and were demanding an investigation. They would be appeased, said Goebbels, only if Roehm, the head of the brownshirts, were also killed.

Hitler nodded, absently. Then he picked up a phone and called the prison in Munich. He told an SS man that Roehm should be asked to commit suicide. Only if he refused, Hitler said, should he be killed.

He put down the phone. He had written the death certificate of one of his oldest comrades. Face ashen, sweat glistening along his forehead, he walked back to the party.

In Munich an SS officer walked into Roehm's cell. The scar-faced Roehm was sitting dejectedly on a bed, naked to the waist. The SS man placed a gun on the table, glanced meaningfully at Roehm, then walked out the door, slamming it behind him.

He and another SS man stood outside the cell for ten minutes.

They heard no shot. They walked into the cell. Roehm still sat on the bed, the gun on the table.

"Roehm, make yourself ready!" an SS gunman shouted. The other pulled a trigger. The gun exploded once, then twice, and Roehm crashed to the floor, blood spurting from gaping holes in his chest. He moaned, "My Fuehrer, my Fuehrer. . . ." The SS man stood over him and drilled a third shot into his head. The moans stopped.

The next day Hitler spoke to the German Reichstag as the nation listened on the radio. He told them that "sixty-one traitors," including nineteen high-ranking storm troopers, had been shot. Years later a Nazi confessed that in that bloody weekend—the Night of the Long Knives, as it would be called—the SS had exterminated "more than a thousand."

"For the last twenty-four hours," Hitler said slowly, "I became the supreme court of the German people. . . . If anyone reproaches me and asks me why I did not resort to the regular courts of justice in dealing with these traitors, then all I can say is that in this hour I was responsible for the fate of the German people. . . . I gave the orders to shoot the ringleaders of this treason. . . . Only ruthless and bloody intervention could have halted the spread of this revolt."

The docile Reichstag deputies stood and applauded. They chanted "Heil Hitler!" Goering, smiling, shouted, "We always approve everything our Fuehrer does."

Indeed, from now on, every German—from generals to ordinary citizens—had to approve what the Fuehrer said and did. The terror of the Night of the Long Knives had taught everyone that anyone who affronted Hitler might die.

11

"War Is Life"

The thin-faced young man wearing a cheap suit and scuffed shoes glanced left and right as he walked up the steps of the German Embassy in Paris. He was seventeen-year-old Herschel Grynszpan. A German Jew, he had fled from Hitler's persecutions. His father had stayed in Germany. Herschel had just learned that his father had been sent to a concentration camp by the Nazis. Herschel had decided to avenge the brutalities the Nazis were inflicting on his father.

He knocked at the door of the embassy. A servant opened it. Herschel saw an embassy official walking down a spiral staircase. The Jewish youth whipped out a pistol and jerked the trigger. The official toppled down the stairs, clutching a widening red circle on his chest, and minutes later was dead.

Other embassy officials overpowered Herschel, and the Paris police took him away. Later he was committed to an insane asylum.

Minutes after the shot was fired, Hitler was notified as he sat at his desk in the Chancellery building in Berlin. Leaping to his feet, he began to shout out orders. The murder of a German by a Jew, he decided, would be the excuse he needed to begin what would be called "the final solution"—the annihilation of every Jewish man, woman, and child in Germany.

That night—November 9, 1938—was the beginning of a week of terror for German Jews. SS men and their lackeys, the now-servile storm troopers, burned synagogues. They wrecked, looted, and set fire to Jewish-owned shops. Jewish men and women were kicked, beaten, and dragged by the hair through the streets. More than 20,000 Jews were shipped off to concentration camps, where most would die by torture or in gas chambers. Gray-haired Jewish men and women were forced to clean streets on their hands and knees while storm troopers stood over them, whips in hand. So many Jewish shops were smashed and looted that the terror became known as the Night of the Broken Glass.

"I certainly would not like to be a Jew in Germany," Goering said ominously as he met with other Nazis a few days after the pillaging began. He ordered that the Jews themselves would have to pay for all that broken glass. German Jews were ordered to begin payment of a billion-mark fine.

Jews lined up outside courthouses to pay their share of that huge penalty. Many walked out of the court without a penny in their pockets and went home to hungry families. Others had to sell their businesses to "Aryan" Germans. They were paid in "bonds" that were next to worthless.

In earlier laws signed by Hitler all Jews had been stripped of German citizenship. They could not vote or hold office. Each was required to wear a large yellow Star of David on his or her clothes. Jews were forbidden to sit on park benches. They were not allowed to drive cars. No Jew could marry a person who wasn't a Jew. Stores would not sell food to Jews. Jewish mothers often had to walk for miles to find a farmer who would sell milk for their children. Hotels had put up signs: JEWS NOT ADMITTED. In many small towns posted signs declared: JEWS ENTER THIS PLACE AT THEIR OWN RISK.

Thousands of Jews fled Germany and poured into France, England, and the United States. Most of the Jews in Germany, however, did not have the money to leave. Entire families were torn from their homes, thrown into freight cars, and shipped to concentration camps like Belsen-Bergen and Dachau and Ravensbrück. Desperate mothers threw their babies out of the trains, hoping they would be picked up and cared for—and many were. In the concentration camps men and women—even children— were worked like farm animals, lashed with whips, and beaten with clubs. Thousands died of beatings, torture, or starvation. Others would line up to die in gas chambers as part of Hitler's "final solution."

Hitler also persecuted Christians. "Since my fourteenth year," he once said, "I have felt liberated from the superstitions that the priests teach." He predicted that he would wipe out "the disease of Christianity." He sent to jail any priests, ministers, or nuns who spoke out against the brutalities of the Nazis. He established a National Reich Church. There were no pastors, priests, crucifixes, or Bibles in those churches. He ordered that the Christian cross "be removed from all churches . . . and superseded by the only unconquerable symbol, the swastika." In 1937 an angry Pope Pius XI delivered an encyclical accusing the Nazis of "fundamental hostility to Christ and His Church."

Hitler now reigned as the sole ruler of Germany. On August 2, 1934, the old war hero, President Hindenburg, had died. A few days after Hindenburg's death, the German people voted on whether Hitler should become the country's dictator. Of the 42,000,000 who voted under the eyes of the SS and the Gestapo,

38,000,000 voted yes, only 4,000,000 voted no. At the age of forty-five the former Vienna tramp stood astride a nation of more than 60,000,000 people. "All Germany and all Germans," wrote historian William L. Shirer, "were in his blood-stained hands."

Hitler immediately pressed the army and its generals to his side. Each soldier and officer had to swear an oath—not to God, not to their country, but to Hitler. Again watched by the Gestapo and SS, who had gunned down a general during the Night of the Long Knives, generals and soldiers put up their right hands and declared, "I swear . . . I will render unconditional obedience to Adolf Hitler, the Fuehrer. . . ."

For the ordinary German man, woman, or child, Hitler seemed to be everywhere. Schoolchildren looked up at his framed portrait, those piercing eyes fixed on them, as they shouted, "Heil Hitler!" with arms upraised. Those eyes looked down on workers in factories, on clerks and typists in offices. "A German," historian Louis Snyder wrote in *Hitler and Nazism*, "could scarcely go anywhere without seeing the face of the Fuehrer staring down at him."

At the age of six all children had to join the Hitler Youth organization. On long hikes they shouted, "The Fuehrer is always right" and "Our life for the Fuehrer." Ten-year-old boys stood under the swastika and declared, "In the presence of this blood banner, which represents our Fuehrer, I swear to devote all my energies and my strength to the savior of our country, Adolf Hitler. I am willing and ready to give up my life for him, so help me God."

At fourteen the boys joined the Hitler Youth. They learned how to be soldiers, firing rifles, living in military camps during summer vacation, sneaking across dark fields in night-fighting drills, and marching 15 miles carrying 12-pound packs.

Girls joined the League of German Maidens. They learned

When Hitler came to Paris, he felt Germany at last had avenged its defeat by France and her Allies in World War I. Here he poses proudly in front of the Eiffel Tower.

Below: After the French Army gave up, German troops advanced triumphantly into Paris. In the background is the Arc de Triomphe. While the Germans were proud of their mechanized forces, much of their artillery, as shown here, still was horse-drawn.

Hitler held Benito Mussolini, fascist dictator of Italy, in utmost contempt. And Mussolini was frightened to death of Hitler. But, as here, they tried not to show their true feelings whenever they got together.

Hitler salutes his brownshirts as the Germans prepare to enter Czechoslovakia. The man to the left in front of Hitler is Rudolf Hess, who nearly forty years later would be the last remaining Nazi war criminal still in Spandau Prison.

At the height of his power Hitler leaves the railroad car where he accepted the surrender of French forces.

Hitler had a childlike love of parades. He reviews battalions of the Nazi
youth movement early in the war in Munich when he seemed destined to
conquer most of Europe.

Above left: In 1923, when Hitler was making his first push for power, some thought him a kind of comic character. He doesn't show much self-confidence here, and those about him do not appear in awe.

Left: Hitler had such intensity as a speaker that the effect was almost hypnotic on most of his listeners. Here he addresses a Nazi Party celebration in Nuremberg.

Hitler and his mistress, Eva Braun, during happy days at his mountaintop retreat at Berchtesgaden. The dog at the right is Blondi, Hitler's favorite.

Hoffman aimed his camera at a broken mirror that offered a perfect image of the dictator when Hitler went to an undisclosed German city to attend a party function.

The photograph of Adolf Hitler by Heinrich Hoffman, the dictator's official photographer.

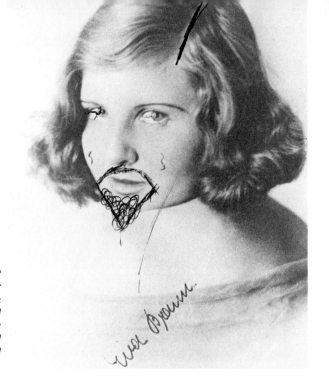

This portrait of Eva Braun at age nineteen, taken from her personal album, was Hitler's favorite of her. Both he and she would meet death by suicide in an underground Berlin bunker when the Third Reich finally collapsed.

This sideview of Hitler was one of the dictator's favorites. It made him look like the great general he felt he truly was.

All photographs courtes of the National Archives

how to swim, folk dance, cook, sew, and work with boys in the fields harvesting crops. In his speeches Hitler told girls "that the most important thing you can do for Germany is to become a mother." A soaring German birthrate would give him the millions of men and women he needed for the future as colonists in the spacious lands he planned to conquer.

Goebbels' propaganda factories churned out millions of books, pamphlets, magazine and newspaper articles depicting Hitler as a demigod. The German people were told that Hitler was all-knowing ("no field of knowledge is strange to him"). Picture books showed him shaking the hands of peasants, tousling the blond hair of "Nordic"-type children, embracing war veterans, chatting with grandmothers and street cleaners, laughing with factory workers. Hitler was at once both the imperial giant and the smiling man of the little people.

What he was really like after he took power and began to assemble German strength for an assault on the world, of course, was something else. André François-Poincet, a French journalist, who knew Hitler, has written:

A Hitler cannot be confined within a simple formula. For my part I knew three facets of his personality, each corre-sponding to a like facet in his nature. His first aspect was one of pallor; his jumbled complexion and vague globular eyes, lost in a dream, lent him an absent, faraway air, the troubled and troubling face of a medium. . . .

The second aspect was animated, colored, swept away by passion. His nostrils would twitch, his eyes dart lightning; he was all violence, impatience of control, lust for domination, abomination of his antagonists, cynical boldness, with a fierce energy ready, at no provocation, to pull down the universe about his ears. This, his "storm and assault" face, was the face of a lunatic.

Hitler's third aspect was that of any naïve, rustic man, dull, vulgar, easily amused, laughing boisterously as he slapped his thigh; a commonplace face without any distinguishing mark, a face like thousands of other faces spread over the face of the earth.

People who spoke with Hitler sometimes saw these three expressions successively. At the beginning of the conversation he seemed not to listen, let alone understand . . . then suddenly, as though a hand had released a lever, he would burst forth into a harangue, uttered in shrill, excited, choleric tones . . . these "fits" might last ten minutes or a half-hour or even three-quarters of an hour. Then, suddenly, the flow stopped; Hitler would fall silent. He seemed exhausted. . . .

These alternate states of excitement and depression . . . ranged from the most devastating fury to the plaintive moanings of a wounded beast. . . . This much is certain: he was no normal human being. He was, rather, a morbid personality, a quasi-madman, a character out of the pages of Dostoyevsky, a man "possessed."

After a few months of sitting behind his desk in the ornate office of the Chancellery Hitler became bored. Often he stayed in the simply furnished bedroom of his apartment,which was also in the Chancellery building, a short walk down the hallway from his office. He read through all the books of Karl May, the Wild West adventure writer who had thrilled him as a boy. He drew architectural plans for a new and lavish Chancellery. When he didn't feel like working, he sat in his private theater and watched adventure movies (a favorite was *Lives of a Bengal Lancer*). Or he slouched in a chair in one of the rooms of the Chancellery, his cronies gathered around him, spouting off as he had done in the old days in Munich and Vienna, when he sat in cafés and beer halls, talking politics. ███ he could talk and know that no

126

one would interrupt, his fawning henchmen saying, "Yes, my Fuehrer," to everything he said. He talked about everything from the cowardice of American soldiers to women's fashions—"the skirts are too long"—to the movies—"they should make more pictures with happy endings"—and even to the newspapers—"put a lot of comics in them and the women and children will buy them." He had opinions on everything. And, according to what Goebbels told the German public, everything he said "is always right. He alone is never mistaken. He is above us all. He is always like a star above us."

The star hated the day-to-day mechanical paperwork of being a leader. When aides thrust thick reports at him to read or brought in dozens of papers for him to sign, he often yawned and brusquely waved them away. One of his favorite sayings was: "A single idea of genius is more valuable than a whole life-time of conscientious office work."

But despite his haphazard concern for details, Hitler's Germany was a bustling place. Some historians have said that if Hitler had suddenly died in 1939, he might have been listed with Bismarck as one of the great German political leaders of all time. He ordered the building of the world's first superhighways—called autobahns. Thousands of German workers happily went to work, laying down hundreds of miles of the broad, winding highways. Meanwhile, with the worldwide depression coming to an end and other countries beginning to demand products from Germany, the wheels of German factories were spinning faster. In bustling German ports, boxes of cameras, optical products, cars, and machinery flowed onto freighters.

Other German factories were hammering out guns, bombs, grenades, tanks, fighter planes, battleships, and heavy bombers. The German army and navy were limited by the Treaty of Versailles to a certain number of weapons and ships. But at Hitler's order German factories were secretly shipping weapons to the army and navy. The army hid tanks, guns, bombs, and airplanes in arsenals, and the navy assembled steel hulls for "passenger ships and freighters" that were really for battleships, destroyers, and submarines.

The frenetic production put money to jingling in the pockets of German workers. Laughing over their steins of beer, they clinked toasts to Hitler and told foreigners, who asked them about their lack of freedom, "Hitler gave us freedom from starvation. Who wants to be free to starve?"

Through Hitler's "Strength Through Joy" program, millions of German families frolicked at seaside resorts or cruised the Mediterranean for as little as $10 a week, most of the cost paid by the government. Hitler had learned from Rome's emperors how to keep the masses happy: "Give them bread and circuses."

The circuses were torchlit mass meetings of the Nazi party, held in Munich, Berlin, Nuremberg, and other German cities, the idea being to instill in Germans a fierce pride and feeling of invincibility. As thousands of voices chanted, "Heil Hitler!" and "Sieg Heil" ("Hail Victory"), Hitler stood on a high platform, arms extended in salute. Above him searchlights probed and stabbed the night sky, and marchers paraded past for hours, flaunting multicolored banners. The red, black, and white swastikas were everywhere. Lights would be extinguished, the stadium suddenly hushed, and the "blood banner"—the swastika—dipped in honor of Nazi "martyrs" who had died for Hitler since the 1923 putsch. Again bands blared, and 100,000 voices roared. Goosestepping soldiers and SS men paraded, heels clicking, bayonets gleaming, flashing arms at Hitler, who stood high above them like some high priest. One visitor from England called one of these demonstrations "the clamor of the barbarians."

Hitler loved such dramatic stagings, just as he was fascinated by the thundering sounds and lightning flashes of Wagner's operas "Look at this fanatical enthusiasm," he once told Goebbels after a mammoth Nazi rally. "You will discover how, in these faces, the same expression has formed, how a hundred thousand men in a movement have become a single type."

He wanted only a single type of German: the fanatical warrior willing to dash to his death for Hitler and the swastika. For he was building a stronger, healthier, united people for one single reason: to send them to war. The world might have overlooked what he had written in *Mein Kampf*, but the goals were engraved in Hitler's mind: first to conquer France, then to turn to the east and swallow up smaller nations as he marched toward the vastness of Russia. "It is not right," he told Germans and the world, "that sixty million Germans should be cooped up in a space so small. We need breathing room, and we shall have it."

To close aides like Goebbels and Goering he said, "The horoscope of the times does not point to peace but to war. War is the ultimate goal of politics. War is the most natural, the most ordinary thing. War is life. All struggle is war."

He took his first step toward war in 1936. He called in his generals and told them that he was about to take what he later called "the greatest chance of my life."

12
"My Nerves, My Nerves, I Must Restore My Nerves!"

Hitler stood up suddenly from his desk and walked across his thickly carpeted office. He stood for a moment under a glittering chandelier, hands clasped behind his back, staring at the carpet. He turned and looked at a clock on his desk. The time was a little after eight o'clock on the evening of March 7, 1936, D-Day for Hitler's first military adventure. Its code name was Operation Winter Exercise, its goal the occupation of the Rhineland.

Some eighteen years earlier defeated German troops had tramped out of France, their rifles left behind according to the terms of the armistice. They had stopped at cities along the Rhine River, places like Cologne, Düsseldorf, and Bonn. The French and British decided to make the area along the Rhine a buffer or protective zone. It was demilitarized: no German soldiers could enter the Rhineland, where they could be poised for another invasion of France. Now Hitler was prepared to challenge England and France by sending his troops into the Rhineland to occupy it.

For days he had worried. What would the French and British do as his truckloads of troops rolled into the Rhineland? The

night before, "I couldn't sleep a wink," he later told Hans Hoff-
mann, his personal photographer. "I asked myself the same question: What will France do? Will she oppose the advance of my
handful of battalions? I know what I would have done, if I had
been the French. I should have struck, and I would not have
allowed a single German soldier to cross the Rhine."

Watching Hitler as he stood in the center of his office were
two of his generals: squat and square-shouldered Werner von
Blomberg; tall and aristocratic-looking Werner von Fritsch. They
understood well why Hitler was pacing with such an agonized
expression. That morning—on Hitler's orders—they had sent
three battalions of German infantry—about 3,000 men—rumbling
across bridges over the Rhine into the Rhineland, covered by
a handful of fighter planes. The Germans marched straight toward
the artillery, tanks, and overpowering might of thirteen French
divisions—more than 100,000 fighting men. If the French decided
to repulse the Germans, they would steamroller over those tiny
three battalions and pour over the bridges into a defenseless
Germany.

General Blomberg cleared his throat. "Perhaps, my Fuehrer,"
he said, hesitantly, "we should pull back the three battalions."

The tall Fritsch nodded in agreement. "We will be blown to
pieces," he said.

Hitler spun and faced them, flushing with rage. "You have lost
your heads and your nerves," he snapped, "but I will not lose
mine. The French, I tell you, will not attack."

Instinctively Hitler sensed the timid mood of the French and
British leaders and people. They dreaded another world war. They
still recalled vividly the bloody slaughter in the trenches of World
War I. In almost every home in England and France was a framed
photo of a loved one who had died—a husband, brother, uncle,
buried now under the red poppies of France. And in every town

in England and France walked one-legged, one-armed, or blinded men who were daily reminders of war's horrors. The people of England and France, Hitler knew, yearned for peace—peace at any price.

"No," he growled to the two generals, "the French will not fight. I am sure of it."

And he was right. The French generals watched Hitler's handful of troops march into the Rhineland and did nothing. The excuse of the French was that an attack by the French "might set off the roar of cannons all along the border between France and Germany and start another bloody war." In England a British statesman shrugged. "After all," he said, sipping his tea, "the Germans are only returning into their own backyard."

But if the French and British had attacked and thrown Hitler's troops out of the Rhineland, the millions of lives lost in World War II might have been saved. ". . . the dictator never could have survived such a fiasco," wrote William L. Shirer in *The Rise and Fall of the Third Reich*. "The defeat almost certainly would have been the end of Hitler after which history might have taken quite a different and brighter turn than it did."

Hitler himself agreed that a French attack would have been a disaster for the Germans. Two days after the occupation he toured the Rhineland in his special train, waving to cheering Germans as church bells pealed, hailed as the "liberator" of this sliver of Germany. "Am I glad it's over!" he told Goebbels as the train whistled back toward Berlin. "Good Lord, am I glad it's gone so smoothly! If the French had marched into the Rhineland against us, we would have had to withdraw with our tail between our legs."

That was Hitler's first small step toward the conquest of Europe. By this time he had secretly built his army from 100,000, the ceiling set by the Treaty of Versailles, to 300,000. Seeing the

British and French back off when he stepped into the Rhineland, Hitler became bold enough to pull the wrappings off his army. The Treaty of Versailles, he told the astonished British and French, "was only a scrap of paper" that he hurled into their faces. His army would continue to balloon to 500,000 men, he announced. And he revealed that he was spending more than $100,000,000—most of it coming from the union dues of German workers—to build a fleet of battleships, fast new submarines, and an armada of Messerschmitt fighters and Junker bombers.

But it was part of Hitler's genius to know instinctively how far he could push the British and French. While he bragged of his gathering military strength, he talked soothingly to them of his desire for peace. "Germany needs peace and desires peace," he shouted in one of his speeches that was broadcast by radio to anxious people all around the world. Germany had wanted only the occupation of the Rhineland, he said, nothing more.

The British and French leaders believed him—for several reasons. One, they wanted to believe him because they recoiled at the thought of war. Two, Hitler's army was a boulder between them and the massive army of Russia's brutal dictator, Joseph Stalin. England and France feared the insidious spread of Russian communism. They welcomed a strong German army facing the Russians.

Hitler plotted his next step. Having bluffed the British and French into a stance of helplessness, he would turn his back on them and look to the east. He would begin his march toward Russia by eating up his old homeland, Austria.

He knew he had to get Italy on his side. For years Italy had been Austria's "bodyguard." Italy, looking north into Austria, did not want to see muzzles of German guns trained on its border.

Hitler began to court the vain, strutting Italian dictator, Benito

Mussolini, who called himself Il Duce. He invited Il Duce to Berlin and welcomed him with cheering crowds and blaring military bands. He hailed Mussolini as "the leading statesman in the world." In private he assured Mussolini that together "we can conquer Russian bolshevism." He dangled in front of Mussolini's eyes the lure of millions of square miles of Russian farm lands, a place of opportunity for Italians now squeezed into crowded cities. And he reminded Mussolini that they were political brothers. Both believed in a powerful dictator who dangled people, labor unions, and corporations like puppets on strings. Fascism, a name first given to Mussolini's political philosophy, now was also being used to describe Hitler's Nazism. By 1936 Hitler had won Mussolini over to his side. The two signed "A Pact of Steel," promising that one would come to the aid of the other in the event of war. Radio and newspaper commentators said the countries were two wheels joined by one axle or axis—and Italy and Germany soon became known as the Axis Powers.

With Italy no longer standing over Austria as a bodyguard, Hitler convened his top generals on the evening of November 5, 1937. At one end of a long brown table in a reception room in Hitler's new Chancellery—as ornate as a king's palace, it had been built at a cost of some $10,000,000—sat the fat Goering, now chief of the air force. Medals dangled from the chest of his tailored uniform. Nearby sat Generals Blomberg and Fritsch. Also at the table were Admiral Erich Raeder and General Wilhelm Keitel, both so anxious to please Hitler—each with the hope he could command the navy and army—that they had become fawning yes-men.

Standing at the head of the table, Hitler began to tell them what Goering knew and what the others had come to suspect: he was building a juggernaut that would roar out of Germany to

135

conquer country after country, just as he had promised in *Mein Kampf*. His first target, he said, was Austria. Then he would unleash his war machine against another country on the east—Czechoslovakia.

Goering, Keitel, and Raeder were among the generals and admirals who applauded. But Blomberg and Fritsch stood up and argued that it would be folly for the German army to plunge eastward against Austria and Czechoslovakia. From the west, they argued, the British and the French would come crashing down on Germany's back, which would be stripped of its border guards, every soldier having been sent to the east for the thrust against Austria and the Czechs.

Hitler sneered. He pointed at Blomberg and Fritsch. "You are the same men," he rasped in his hollow, vibrating voice, "who told me the French would attack when we took the Rhineland. You lost your nerve. You are losing it again. We will march east, and the French and British will not attack from the west. They are worms who are afraid of a good fight."

Hitler decided that Fritsch and Blomberg were obstacles in his way. He dismissed them and announced over the radio to the German people, "From now on I take over personally the command of the whole armed forces." He would give orders to Goering for his air force, to the toadying Keitel for the army, to the anxious-to-please Raeder for the navy.

From 1937 and on into 1938 Goebbels' propaganda bureau trumpeted Germany's claim to annexing Austria. All over the world people read and listened to a litany of lies and half-lies that would become a familiar routine as Hitler made claim to country after country. Of Austria's 8,000,000 people, about 2,000,000 spoke German. Those 2,000,000, lied Goebbels, were being persecuted by Austria: beaten, tortured, jailed, killed. Germany wanted to save those persecuted Germans. It wanted only to annex those areas of Austria where most of the inhabitants were German.

The pressure built on Austria's leaders, who were fearful Hitler's legions would burst into their country at any moment. Finally, on a frosty winter morning in February, 1938, Austria's Chancellor, the courtly, soft-spoken, forty-one-year-old Kurt von Schuschnigg, arrived at the Eagle's Nest, as Hitler called his mountaintop castle in the Bavarian Alps. The Eagle's Nest sat above the town of Berchtesgaden where he and Geli had lived during the 1920's.

A foreign newspaperman once described the Eagle's Nest:

From afar the extraordinary place . . . looked like a sort of observatory or hermitage, perched at an altitude of over six thousand feet. . . . A hairpin road, about ten miles long, cut boldly through the rocks, wound upward. . . . The road led to the entrance of a long underground passageway dug deep into the soil. . . . At the end of this corridor a roomy copper-lined elevator awaited the visitor; its shaft, hewn vertically through the rock, rose over three hundred seventy feet to the level on which the Fuehrer had his dwelling. I was ushered into a squat, solid building, which consisted of a gallery with Roman pillars, an immense glassed-in rotunda. . . . To look out in any direction over the endless panorama of mountains was like looking down from an airplane. . . .

When Schuschnigg entered Hitler's office on the second floor of the Eagle's Nest, he looked out through the huge picture window—said to be the world's largest—at a breath-catching view of the mountains of three nations, Germany, Austria, and Italy. Dressed in the formal clothes of a diplomat, the Austrian began with a polite compliment to his host: The view, he said, was extraordinary.

"We did not gather here to speak of the fine view or the

weather," Hitler snapped at the astonished Schuschnigg. Then, for an hour, he poured invective and threats at his visitor. He accused Austria of "a continuous betrayal" of Germany. The Austrian tried to interject a protest, but Hitler trampled over his words. "I have a historic mission and I am going to fulfill it because Providence has appointed me to do so. . . . I have traveled the hardest road that ever a German had to travel, and I have accomplished the greatest things in German history that ever a German was destined to accomplish. . . . I have only to give an order to my generals and in one single night all your ridiculous army will be blown to bits."

Then he became conciliatory. He didn't want to destroy the land of his birth. Schuschnigg could save Austria, Hitler said. He handed the Chancellor a document. If Schuschnigg signed the document, Hitler would not march into Austria.

Schuschnigg picked up the document and began to read it. His eyes widened. The document demanded that an Austrian Nazi, Dr. Artur von Seyss-Inquart, he appointed the head of the Austrian police. Another Nazi was to be given command of the Austrian army. As he read the document, Schuschnigg realized that this was what one historian later called "the death warrant of Austria."

"Austria has three days to sign this," Hitler warned, eyes fixed on Schuschnigg's face. "There is nothing to discuss. You will either sign it within three days or I will order the march into Austria."

Hitler went on staring at the shocked Schuschnigg. Austria had no one to turn to, he warned. Neither England, France, nor Italy would rush to its aid. Austria stood alone against German might.

A despondent Schuschnigg left the Eagle's Nest and returned by train to Vienna. There he and the Austrian President, Wilhelm Miklas, sadly signed the document.

Immediately the new Nazi chief of police released Nazi ter-rorists from jails. They led German mobs who tore down the Austrian flags in dozens of cities and towns and hoisted the swastika. The mobs chanted for the ouster of Schuschnigg and the appointment of Seyss-Inquart as Austria's Chancellor. For three weeks Austria bubbled with turmoil while German radio propagandists blared more lies that Germans in Austria were being killed. On that pretext Hitler ordered Operation Otto into effect, declaring in his order, "I intend to invade Austria with armed forces in order to establish constitutional conditions and to prevent further outrages against the pro-German population."

A frantic Schuschnigg radioed England and Italy, begging for help. Mussolini wired back that he doubted Hitler would invade Austria. England's Prime Minister, the tall and urbane Neville Chamberlain, stroked his mustache and told the Austrians he could see no indication of German aggression.

Then Mussolini told an aide to call Hitler to tell him the Austrian question was no longer any concern of Italy's.

Hitler almost fell to his knees in gratitude. "Please tell Mussolini that I shall never forget this. Never, never, never, come what may," he told Mussolini's aide. "Whenever he should be in need or in danger, he can be sure that I will stick with him, rain or shine, come what may. . . ."

Goering, meanwhile, had concocted a ruse. He ordered the Austrian Nazis to send a telegram to Berlin begging Hitler's troops to invade Austria and save German families from being butchered by anarchists. The Austrian Nazi told Goering the telegram would be sent immediately.

"You don't even have to send the telegram," Goering said, laughing.

Goering wrote the telegram in Berlin. He showed it to a smiling Hitler. Now Hitler had the excuse he needed to send his troops, tanks, and planes swarming into Austria. On the night of March 11, 1938, German tanks and trucks rumbled into Austria. The Austrian troops stood aside and let them pass, under orders from their Nazi commander not to fight. In town after town the invading troops were greeted by flower-throwing pro-German crowds.

In Berlin, though, Hitler bit his lip anxiously. He worried over what the crack Czech army might do. After Hitler occupied Austria, the Czechs would face German guns on three sides. Hitler feared the Czechs might rush into Austria and blunt the Nazi drive.

On that night of March 11, as German soldiers crossed the border into Austria, Goering slipped into a party in Berlin attended by formally dressed diplomats and jeweled women in evening dresses. He took aside the Czech ambassador to Germany and spoke to him in a corner in smooth, nonchalant tones. The invasion of Austria, he told the diplomat, "is only a family affair between us and the Austrians. The Czechoslovakian government has nothing to fear from Germany."

The Czech diplomat said he would have to notify his government in Prague. He went to a nearby telephone. A few minutes later he came back and told the waiting, anxious Goering that the Czechs would not go into Austria to stop the Germans. Smiling, Goering rushed off to tell Hitler the good news.

The next day a shiny-eyed, triumphant Hitler was driven into Austria. Huge crowds cheered him as his car moved slowly through the jammed streets of Braunau, where he had been born forty-nine years before. In Linz, the town whose streets he had once walked at night while dreaming of his future, more than 100,000 people roared for him as he stood on the balcony of the City Hall. Tears ran down his face.

Many Austrians looked the other way, however, as they saw brown-shirted storm troopers dragging and kicking Jewish men and women in the streets. Old Jewish men were forced to scrub sidewalks. Former Chancellor Schuschnigg was arrested by SS men and ordered to clean their toilets. Then he was thrown into a concentration camp from which he was freed, seven long years later, emaciated but alive, by American GIs.

In Vienna Hitler shook hands with an old friend, Gustl Kubizek, whom he had not seen since he fled their apartment on Stumper Alley here in Vienna almost thirty years earlier. They talked for hours, and Hitler reminded Gustl what he had predicted on the Feinberg so long ago; that one day he would be a world ruler.

Indeed, he had come far, once a beggar in this city, now the ruler of an expanding empire of more than 70,000,000. But after a few days he became depressed. "I do not have long to live," he often told intimates. He worried constantly that he had cancer or some other dread disease. He swallowed pills and spoke often of his "damaged" nerves. "My nerves, my nerves," he once exclaimed. "I must restore my nerves. . . . Worries, worries, worries, insane worries; it truly is a tremendous burden of worries." He feared he would be killed by an assassin's bullet before he could, as he said, "solve all the problems that had to be solved, for only I can do it. The men who came after me will not be able to do it. . . . Oh, if only my health were good!"

The day after his triumphal entry into Vienna, he was stricken by stomach cramps (for all his life he had been troubled and embarrassed by flatulence). He told his doctors that his intestinal weaknesses were signs of stomach cancer. Fearing cancer, he did not smoke, drink alcohol or even coffee or tea. He refused to eat meat, calling it the "food of the bloodthirsty." And often, when stricken by cramps and intestinal upsets, he sunk even deeper into one of his depressed, lethargic moods, moving as though in a trance, "dozing like a crocodile in the Nile mud," as one secretary put it.

Then he would suddenly burst out of that mood and display a

141

furious energy, bouncing with new plans, "as fresh as a colt in pasture," as he once told Goering.

He would soon need all that energy. For his next target was one that would make his generals wince. He aimed to destroy the proud young democratic state of Czechoslovakia, whose people had more freedom than any country in central Europe. The nation was guarded by a tough, well-trained army, crouched behind concrete forts. That nation and that army were soon to be betrayed—by friends.

13

"We Will Arrest Hitler . . ."

The Junker airplane, the black swastika painted on its silver fuselage, banked steeply to the right, one wingtip dipping toward the ground. Then it straightened and began to climb, its three engines roaring as the propellors bit into the cool night air. Hitler stared out the window at the rows of blinking lights below him. His plane had just taken off from the Munich airport on this evening of May 28, 1938, some two months after his conquest of Austria.

During the past few weeks he had sat brooding at the Eagle's Nest. He had won two bloodless victories in a row in the Rhineland and then in Austria. Germans were calling him a genius who was pushing out the boundaries of Germany without firing a shot. But Hitler had again sunk into one of his blackest moods. It was as though his jangling nerves screamed for the action of war instead of the bluffing and scheming of the past two years. Yet, when Hitler had reached for the saber during the Rhineland crisis and the Austrian crisis, his nerves had twitched. Like the moth to the flame, he was attracted to a war that could consume him.

But now, he told himself as the Junker droned toward Berlin, he had made a decision. He swore that he would not be swayed from that decision, even though he knew the decision could mean the start of World War II.

A few hours later the Junker's wheels touched down on Berlin's Tempelhof Airport. Hitler walked from the plane to a waiting black limousine as soldiers snapped to attention. He stepped into the limousine, then turned to his chief secretary, the hard-eyed, piggish-faced Martin Bormann, and told Bormann to order all his generals to meet with him in the reception room of the Chancellery the next morning.

The next morning Hitler strode into the reception room under rows of glittering chandeliers. The generals rose and shouted, "Heil Hitler!" Hitler thrust out his right arm in the Nazi salute. The generals sat down, their chairs scraping the marble floor.

Hitler stared at them for several moments. Then, in clipped words, he declared, "It is my unshakable will that Czechoslovakia be wiped off the map." He turned to a large chart that had been mounted on a tripod stand. On the top of the chart were the words "Operation Green." Hitler pointed to the chart and began to outline it. He concluded: "With these plans, we will smash Czechoslovakia. . . ."

That evening two of Hitler's top generals, General Ludwig Beck and Field Marshall Walther von Brauchitsch, talked in the latter's office about Operation Green. Beck, tall, and thin-lipped, spoke with the cool preciseness of a college professor. The chesty Brauchitsch, looking somewhat like a beer barrel, loved to strut in front of troops but could be reduced to shaking by one of Hitler's stormy rages. Supposedly the commander of the army, Brauchitsch had become only a messenger boy who delivered Hitler's orders to his generals. Now, as he sat behind his desk, Brauchitsch's face paled while he listened to Beck rip apart Hitler's Operation Green.

"There are two facts that are unpleasant but logical," Beck said in his dry fashion. "Hitler must be made to realize that Operation Green will result in a defeat for Germany worse than 1918."

Brauchitsch, fiddling nervously with the buttons of his tunic, asked why.

First of all, said Beck, the Czech army was tough, well armed, and entrenched behind forts facing the German border. Germany would have to hurl all of its 1,000,000 troops at those forts to sweep over them—and, even then, might be stopped.

Secondly, Beck went on, pacing the large office, Germany's back would be unprotected against an attack by the French. "I know the French did not attack when we marched into the Rhineland, but this time they will. They must. They have no choice."

Brauchitsch nodded. The British and the French had signed a treaty guaranteeing to attack any country that attacked Czechoslovakia.

The stubby field marshal stood up and walked to a window. "But what can I do?" he asked Beck with a kind of moan. "How can I convince the Fuehrer that Operation Green will fail?"

"You must!" snapped Beck.

Brauchitsch winced at the thought of braving one of Hitler's rages. Beck, watching him, began to realize that Brauchitsch would not, or could not, argue Hitler out of commencing Operation Green.

Until then only a few Germans had banded together to conspire against Hitler. The Gestapo, its ears seemingly in every room, had caught most of those plotters. They were beaten, tortured, or killed in concentration camps. Other Germans despaired of ever toppling Hitler. William L. Shirer wrote, "How could a tiny group . . . rise up in revolt against the machine guns, the tanks and the flame throwers of the SS?"

But the army's generals had the troops and the firepower to smash Hitler's Gestapo and SS army. Up to now the generals had had no reason to oppose Hitler. He had built their army to more than 1,000,000 troops and given them enough tanks, planes, and artillery to make it the most modern in the world. While the French, British, and American armies were plodding models of World War I vintage, equipped to fight only trench warfare, the German army—with its motorized panzer tanks and armored cars—had become a speedy juggernaut, what Hitler would call "a bolt of iron lightning."

Now, however, General Beck feared that this army would be sandwiched between the French and Czechs and destroyed. Other generals agreed with him in midnight candlelit conferences in small hotel rooms, held secretly to be safe from the Gestapo. One of the generals was Franz Halder, a crisp, professorial commander. He had called Hitler "that criminal madman and bloodsucker." When General Beck retired from the army in the summer of 1938 as a silent protest against Operation Green, General Halder became the ringleader of the anti-Hitler conspirators. And by the late summer of 1938 they had a plan: General Halder would order army troops to arrest Hitler forty-eight hours before the start of Operation Green.

But General Halder had to be sure of one thing: that the British and the French would do what they had promised in their treaty with Czechoslovakia. They had to attack Germany when Hitler attacked the Czechs. The generals knew that a revolt against Hitler would be supported by the German troops and civilians only if an avalanche of Allied troops was pouring across the border into Germany. General Halder sent secret messages to the British and the French. One stated emphatically: "The immediate intervention by France and England to aid Czechoslovakia will bring about the downfall of Hitler."

To the amazement of the German generals, the French and British leaders—the stocky, black-haired Édouard Daladier and tall, willowy, mustached Neville Chamberlain—seemed to cast aside their messages as not important. Daladier and Chamberlain seemed much more interested in trying to give Hitler whatever he wanted so that he would not attack the Czechs and drag them into the world war they feared.

In his diplomatic talks with the Czechs, Hitler had demanded that Germany be given the Sudetenland, an 11,000-square-mile portion of Czechoslovakia that was rich with coal mines and dotted with chemical factories. Hitler needed the coal and the factories to fuel his war machine. And the Sudetenland was studded with the forts that protected the remainder of Czechoslovakia. If Hitler's troops could be handed over those forts without firing a shot, they could easily flow into the rest of the country.

The Sudetenland was populated by 4,000,000 people, 1,000,000 of them German-speaking. Goebbels' propagandists trumpeted to the world made-up stories of Germans being slaughtered in the Sudetenland. These "barbarous" acts must be stopped, warned the German radio, repeating the strategy that had worked so well against Austria, "or the German army will march into the Sudetenland to save German men, women, and children from slaughter."

Late in the summer of 1938 the slender, soft-spoken president of Czechoslovakia, Eduard Benes, began to worry that he would be abandoned by his British and French allies, who seemed to lack the stomach to attack Hitler. Reluctantly, Benes called in the leader of the Nazi Party in Czechoslovakia.

"Write out what you want," Benes told the Nazi. "Whatever your demands, we accept."

The exultant Nazi telegraphed Berlin: THEY HAVE GIVEN US

147

EVERYTHING! The Sudetenland, as Hitler had demanded, would be made a puppet state, its strings pulled by Hitler.

A few days earlier, however, Hitler had received a message from Chamberlain asking for a meeting to discuss the Sudetenland. Hitler sensed that he could get even more by talking with Chamberlain. He telegraphed back to the Czech Nazis: Make up some excuse and refuse to talk any longer with Benes.

The sixty-nine-year-old Chamberlain flew to the Eagle's Nest at Berchtesgaden. Patiently he listened as Hitler demanded not the independent state that he had originally sought, but the handing over of the Sudetenland to be swallowed up into Germany. The Germans would operate the coal mines, chemical factories, and forts of the Sudetenland on their own, without having to share them with the Czechs.

A courtly and naïve man, Chamberlain was impressed by Hitler. "In spite of the hardness and ruthlessness that I thought I saw in his face," he said later to one of his aides, "I got the impression that here was a man who could be relied upon when he had given his word."

Chamberlain flew back to London and talked by telephone with Daladier in Paris. A few days earlier a French general had confidently told Daladier that the French and the Czechs outnumbered the Germans three to one. "The Germans," said the French general, "would be caught in a nutcracker's squeeze between the Czechs and the French."

A German general, years later, agreed. "With only five divisions on the western front against a hundred French divisions," he said, "the Germans would have been overwhelmed at their back. And the Czechs would have held the Germans at bay on the point of their forts while the Germans were overrun from the rear by the onrushing French 100 divisions." And, William L. Shirer wrote, "That would have been the end of Hitler and the Third Reich."

But Daladier and Chamberlain hesitated to come to the aid of the Czechs. They kept imagining German planes bombing the beautiful cities of London and Paris. "And what for?" Chamberlain asked his Cabinet. "To protect a faraway country like Czechoslovakia?"

Daladier and Chamberlain decided to give Hitler what he had demanded: The Sudetenland would be gobbled up by Germany. They looked away from the pained, betrayed faces of their Czech allies.

Chamberlain flew back to Germany. He sat down with Hitler in a hotel room overlooking the Rhine. Facing Hitler across a small table, Chamberlain smilingly told Hitler that the French and British had agreed to his demands.

Hitler stared, amazed. "Do I understand," he asked, "that the British, French, and Czech governments have agreed to the transfer of the Sudetenland from Czechoslovakia to Germany?"

Chamberlain's eyes twinkled. "Yes," he said.

Hitler could not believe it had been so easy. Instinctively he grabbed for more. He told Chamberlain that he wanted the Sudetenland right away—by October 1, only eight days hence. Otherwise, he warned, he would invade Czechoslovakia.

Chamberlain's long face flushed angrily. He began to see how ruthless Hitler really was—and why he couldn't be trusted.

Hitler quickly tried to soothe Chamberlain. This would be his last request, he assured Chamberlain. He would ask for nothing more. And Chamberlain then would have what he had sought—peace.

A confused Chamberlain flew back to London to confer with his Cabinet and the French. All around the globe people wondered if they stood on the brink of World War II as the days approached Hitler's October 1 deadline.

In Washington President Franklin D. Roosevelt wrote a letter to Hitler appealing to him not to invade Czechoslovakia and begin a war. In Prague the Czech government ordered its army of 1,000,000 to man its forts and await the German charge. In London schoolchildren were bused to the country to be safe from German bombers. In Paris French troops, clutching bayoneted rifles, stood on trucks that roared east toward the German border.

In Berlin General Halder conferred with other generals. "I have arranged with certain people in the high command," he told them in his wood-paneled office, "that I will be given forty-eight hours' advance warning of Hitler's final order to attack the Czech border. . . . With the Berlin troops we will overpower Hitler's SS bodyguards and arrest him. Immediately he will be tried before a People's Court. I, myself, will have convinced enough generals before the trial—and I will show the German people during the trial—that Hitler had tried to involve Germany in a war that it would inevitably lose and bring on the hardships of 1918. We will prove he is no longer mentally competent to be the head of the German state." The generals, he added, would take power, then begin the process of setting up a new German democracy.

The next day Halder learned that Hitler had ordered the invasion to begin on September 30. That was only forty-eight hours away. Halder and the other generals decided to arrest Hitler on the twenty-ninth.

On the morning of the twenty-eighth Hitler sat in his office in the Chancellery. Nazi flags were mounted around his desk. His face was pale and glistened wetly. All along he had cockily told Goebbels, Goering, and his other lieutenants that the French and British would back away from war. "War!" he had chortled. "The word makes their hands tremble. At the last moment the British and French will stand by and watch us smash the Czechs to bits."

Now, as telegrams poured onto his desk from his ambassadors

in France and England, telling of the massing of Allied troops, he was not so sure. The Allied armies were on his left and the Czechs on his right, two giant hands that could smash his army like an egg in one loud, awful clap. And from Washington his ambassador had cabled that the Americans would "send tanks, guns, and planes from their factories to the British and French armies."

Then, to Hitler's smiling relief, came another telegram—from Chamberlain. The British and French proposed a conference of the leaders of Britain, France, Germany, and Italy. In that conference, the message assured him, he would get everything he wanted—"without war and without delay."

The next day the four leaders flew to Munich and sat down around a long table—Italy's glowering Mussolini, the pensive Daladier, a weary Chamberlain, and a triumphant Hitler. Outside the room the anxious Czechs waited to hear their fate. They soon learned that nearly half of Czechoslovakia, including the rich Sudetenland, would be handed over to Germany. Hitler's troops would march into their half of Czechoslovakia in the morning.

In Berlin the German generals stared at each other with amazement when they heard of the Munich agreement. They couldn't believe the Allies had caved in to Hitler rather than risk a war they were certain to win.

"The impossible has happened," growled one general. "The revolt against Hitler is done for. The troops would never revolt against a victorious Fuehrer."

And years later another German general said, "Chamberlain saved Hitler."

In Prague President Benes sadly told his people, "We have been deserted by our friends." He could order his army to fight the invading Germans. But he knew the German army would relentlessly move across the country, killing hundreds of thousands with their artillery and heavy bombers. The war would end with Czechoslovakia in ruins. Benes resigned and flew to London, knowing—as quickly happened—that Hitler would soon occupy all of his once-proud democracy.

All across Germany, meanwhile, people exulted over Hitler's newest conquest. In six months he had added the territory of two countries and more than 10,000,000 people to his expanding Third Reich—without the loss of one German life. Whatever Hitler wanted, Germans now believed, he could get—without war.

Chamberlain flew from Munich to London. Thousands of people, ecstatic that there would be no war, roared for him at the airport. Waving an umbrella, he told the cheering crowds that he had come back "with peace for our time."

But Munich would become—to a generation of Americans, British, and French—a symbol of the appeasement of Hitler's insatiable appetite for territory.

In London's House of Commons a stout, beefy-faced speaker arose and told his fellow members that Munich was "a total and unmitigated defeat." Then, in rich and rolling tones, his eyes flashing, he sounded a warning that "a time of reckoning" was coming for Hitler, a time when free men would stand and face down his bullying.

The speaker was Winston Spencer Churchill, and that time of reckoning was about to begin.

14
"The Whole World Would Laugh at My Bluff"

The uniformed messenger walked quickly into Hitler's office. He saluted the Fuehrer, then placed a telegram on his desk. Hitler snatched up the telegram and began to read it. His face purpled. His voice a high screech, he shouted, "I'll cook them a stew they'll choke on."

The telegram, from London, was a report by the German ambassador on a speech made a day earlier, on March 31, 1939, by Neville Chamberlain. In the months after Germany had swallowed up the other half of helpless Czechoslovakia, Chamberlain had come to see the real Hitler. In the last few weeks Hitler had been demanding the return of Danzig, a port on the Baltic Sea, to Germany. It had been taken from Germany and given to Poland by the Treaty of Versailles. Poland's leaders refused to give Danzig—and a corridor of land leading from Germany to the port—to the Germans. In his speech Chamberlain warned Hitler that if he attacked Poland, England would march to Poland's rescue.

Hitler was determined to use Danzig as a pretext to attack

Poland. "Danzig is not the subject of the dispute at all," he told his generals. "It is a question of expanding our living space toward the east. There is no question of sparing Poland, and we are left with the decision: to attack Poland at the first suitable opportunity."

He paused. "I shall make up a reason for starting the war. Never mind whether the reason is believable or not. Afterward, when he has won, the victor will not be asked whether he told the truth or not. In starting and waging a war, it is not who is right that matters, but who is victorious."

Then, pounding fist on palm, he shouted, "Close your hearts to pity! Act brutally! The stronger man is right!"

In the spring of 1939 Hitler told his generals, "Further success can no longer be attained without the shedding of blood. Victories without blood are demoralizing to one's troops."

Late in May, 1939, he ordered his generals to prepare Operation White—the attack on Poland. The date for invasion was set for September 1.

But first, Hitler knew, he had to divide his enemies to conquer them. In World War I the Germans had fought on two fronts, struggling against the British-French-American allies on the west while battling the Russians in the east. World War I had taught Hitler how a two-front war could end with Germany crushed between two foes.

If he attacked Poland, he reasoned, the French and English probably would stand by and watch—as they had done six months earlier, when he swept Czechoslovakia into his bag. But if the French and English did attack, he could rush millions of Italian troops—the Pact of Steel had made Mussolini his sworn partner in case of war—into his forts along the German-French border. While the Italians pinned down the Allies in the west, he could sweep over the weak Polish army in the east with his motorized juggernaut. Then he could turn his army around to join the Italians in facing the Allies in the west.

But there was one danger: that Russia's mammoth army would spill over the Polish border to join with the Poles in stopping him. Then he would be mired down in a two-front war. Somehow he had to ensure that the Russians did not attack him.

Ever since 1920 Hitler—as a street orator, as a Nazi leader, now as Germany's dictator—had screamed of the horrors of "Russian bolshevism" and warned of "Communist butcher squads." He had soared to power by telling the German people that he and his Nazis were their bulwarks against the red tide of communism that could "drown them in blood."

Now, secretly, he began to work for a treaty that would astound the world—a treaty of peace with Communist Russia and its mustached, ruthless dictator, Joseph Stalin. One day he startled Goebbels and a few other of his cronies when he said, offhandedly, that he and Stalin were alike in many ways, having risen from being poor to stand as world leaders. One of his henchmen protested, pointing out that Stalin had been a bank robber.

Hitler brushed aside the protest. "If Stalin did commit a bank robbery," he said coolly, "it was not to fill his own pockets but to help his party and his movement. You cannot consider that bank robbery."

All during the summer of 1939, while Hitler rubbed his hands anxiously, his Foreign Minister, a former liquor salesman named Joachim von Ribbentrop, shuttled between Berlin and Moscow. Hitler told Ribbentrop that the peace treaty with Russia had to be signed before September 1, the jumping-off date for the invasion of Poland.

To intimates he explained why he wanted war as soon as possible. "I am fifty years old, but no one knows how long I shall live.

Essentially, all depends on me, because of my political talents. Probably no one will ever again have the confidence of the German people that I have. . . . My life, therefore, is a factor of great value. But I can be eliminated at any time by sudden death —no one in my family had a long life—or I could be killed by a criminal or an idiot. . . . No one knows how long I shall live. Therefore, the inevitable conflict is better now."

During that summer he constantly waved aside the objections of his generals that the English and French would finally attack in the west. "Our enemies are men who are below average," he insisted, "no masters, no men of action." But even if the Allies did attack Germany's west wall, he said, Mussolini's Italian army would be massed to check them while he wiped out Poland.

Other worried generals pointed out to Hitler that the German army carried only a six-week supply of ammunition. That would be used up, they said, against the Poles.

But Hitler knew the strategy of modern war—and the weaknesses of his enemies—far better than most of his generals. The generals thought of a war being fought in the trenches, two sides hurling bombs and bullets at each other until one side collapsed of exhaustion.

Hitler dreamed of lightning-fast wars. His new mechanized panzer units—huge tanks and swift armored cars—could surround and destroy slow-moving infantry and cavalry troops on horseback. (In German *Panzer* means coat of mail or armor.) Hitler was planning on winning what would soon be called blitzkriegs, or lightning wars, with his panzer divisions.

First, he would blitzkrieg Poland. Then he would turn around to face the west, while he replenished his ammunition with a blitz—or lightning-fast—effort by his munitions factories. Another blitz would destroy France. Finally, he would turn his armies around once more for a final blitz—a lightning stroke at the throat of the Russian bear. Once that bear had fallen, the vastness of Russia would be his—the breathing space he had yearned for all these years since *Mein Kampf*.

On the morning of August 24, 1939, only seven days before the planned assault on Poland, Hitler and Stalin astounded their own people and the world. They announced a nonaggression treaty. Both promised not to attack the other. Russia would send coal, oil, and grain to fuel the German war machine, and Germany would ship machines for Russia's factories and farms.

Now, with Russia neutralized, Hitler anxiously waited as the hours ticked by toward September 1. Then, one morning, came devastating news: A letter from Mussolini informed Hitler that Italy was not yet ready for war.

"The news of Mussolini's defection hit Hitler's Chancellery like a bombshell," an aide said later. Pacing his office, hands behind his back, Hitler feared that without the Italians to hold back the Allies, he could be overwhelmed from the rear when he attacked Poland.

Desperate, Hitler didn't know what to do. "I can't back down on my demands for Danzig," he told a gloomy Goering. "The whole world would laugh at my bluff."

Goering suggested sending an emissary to England and France to persuade the Allies not to attack Germany when the Germans invaded Poland. Back came the British-French reply: Hitler would be under a "dangerous illusion" if he thought the Allies would fail to live up to their agreements to help Poland.

Hitler ordered Ribbentrop to talk to the ambassadors from England and France. Hitler himself told the British ambassador that if he got Danzig, he would ask for nothing more. "I will retire to be an artist," Hitler said solemnly, "which is what I have always wanted to be."

Like a child begging for a toy, Hitler was pleading: "Give me just this one thing, and I will ask for nothing else."

But he had tried that lie once too often. After returning from

London, a German emissary informed Hitler that the British no longer trusted him. They thought he was a perennial liar.

"Idiots!" Hitler shouted. "Have I ever told a lie in my life?"

None of his Nazi subordinates, of course, had the courage to answer that question.

The German generals were excited when they heard of Hitler's quandary. "Hitler will never dare another world war with England and France," General Halder wrote in his diary, and added, "The Fuehrer is considerably shaken." And a German admiral told a friend, "Hitler will never survive this. . . . Peace has been saved for the next twenty years."

A heat wave baked Europe during those last days of August. German families rowed on lakes or picnicked in the sultry green countryside. So often during the past few years Hitler had pushed them close to the brink of war—only to draw them back at the last moment. They paid little attention to the headlines printed by Goebbels' writers: POLES BURN GERMAN FARMHOUSES and DANZIG GERMANS MURDERED. They had read those stories before—first from Austria, then from Czechoslovakia, but each time Uncle Adolf, as German children had been taught to call him, had spared the country the anguish of war.

His back pressing closer to the wall as September 1 drew near, Hitler decided to offer Poland a sixteen-point proposal to negotiate for the return of Danzig to Germany. The Poles haughtily refused. Emboldened by the promises of Britain and France to attack from the west if Germany invaded Poland, the Polish leaders announced that Poland, "even a Poland abandoned by her allies, is ready to fight and to die alone."

On the afternoon of August 31 a sticky-hot day in Berlin, Hitler dined with Goebbels, Goering, and Himmler. By now, he told them, he was convinced that the English and French would not march against him. "The English and the French," he said, "will leave the Poles in the lurch just as they did the Czechs."

Late that night Operation White began. It began with a fake attack by Germans on a German radio station near the border. The Germans had dressed a concentration-camp prisoner in a Polish army uniform, then killed him and left him on the lawn near the radio station.

"The Poles have attacked Germany," the Berlin radio announced shortly after midnight of September 1, telling of the "attack by murderous Poles" on the station. And at four forty-five that morning of September 1, as dawn lit up the sky. German artillery spat fire and smoke. Shells soared high into the sky and crashed into the midst of Polish infantrymen. The guns of World War II had begun to roar.

That morning Germany awoke to hear Hitler on their radios. Polish soldiers had attacked a German radio station, he announced. And in a strident voice he said that he had no choice "except to meet force with force."

At the Chancellery reports streamed across Hitler's desk that his panzer tanks, covered by screaming Stuka dive-bombers (they had been fitted, at Hitler's suggestion, with sirens to terrify ground troops) had smashed through Polish cavalrymen. The Poles fought bravely, but men on horseback were blown from their saddles by armored cannon and machine guns. Miles of countryside were littered with dead horses and the bloody corpses of Polish soldiers.

Friday, the first, went by; then Saturday, the second, and as Germany drove deeper into Poland, the French and British had not moved. Hitler was sure England and France had backed away from Poland. But on a bright Sunday morning September 3, a messenger walked into the Chancellery, carrying a note from the British ambassador.

Inside a room adjacent to Hitler's office, slouched on a couch, the fat Hermann Goering watched the messenger walk into Hitler's office. Goering frowned. By now he was a millionaire; he had plundered the treasures of museums in Austria and Czechoslovakia and robbed millions of marks from the treasuries of corporations whose Jewish owners had been murdered. He wanted no war that would disrupt his lucrative rackets. For weeks he had warned Hitler and Ribbentrop that they were pushing the English and French too far.

Inside Hitler's office the messenger saluted and handed the British note to Hitler. Hitler scanned it quickly. It was an ultimatum: Germany had to pull back its troops from Poland or England would declare war.

Hitler glared at Ribbentrop. It had been Hitler who had said, over and over, that England would leave the Poles in the lurch. But now he tried to pin the blame for war with England on Ribbentrop.

"What now?" he snapped sarcastically at his Foreign Minister.

The dull-witted Ribbentrop did not seem to notice the sarcasm. "I assume," he said matter-of-factly, "that the French will hand in a similar ultimatum within the hour."

The French did, as Goering cursed. 'Now," he growled at Ribbentrop, "you've got your damned war." And later, sitting in the tense atmosphere of Hitler's office, the dictator staring pensively outside at the garden, Goering muttered, "If we lose this war, then God have mercy on us."

That evening, dressed in a field-gray uniform, black boots, and a general's visored cap pulled down over his eyes, Hitler boarded a private train. As the train roared out of Berlin, streaking for the front in Poland, Hitler was swept by alternate moods of depression and elation. "Now all my work crumbles," he said dejectedly to Rudolf Hess, who had helped him begin that work at Landsberg Prison. But swollen by a sudden intake of optimism, he cheerfully told his valet that the British and French would "break their teeth" on the wall of forts he had built along Germany's west border. The west wall, manned by a handful of Germans, had to hold firm or Hitler's main armies would be cut down from the rear.

Britain and France, however, would not break their teeth on that west wall. To the amazement of later historians, they did not even take a hard bite.

15
"The Greatest Generalissimo of All Times"

Hitler stepped off the train, his black boots crunching into the ashy dirt of the railroad bed. An early-morning fog swirled around his long streamlined train as he peered into the mists. A hole broke through the fog, and Hitler made out plumes of smoke rising from a nearby Polish city.

A general strode up to him, saluted, then presented a large map. An aide rushed forward, and Hitler sat down in a camp chair. He scanned the map.

"The Poles have been driven back all along this line, my Fuehrer," the general said, pointing with his finger. "Our troops are closing in on Warsaw. The Polish army is in full retreat."

Hitler smiled. Other generals came to report that Hitler's blitzkrieging juggernaut had swallowed the Polish army between its iron jaws. And Hitler's heavy bombers were pounding Warsaw and other cities into smoking rubble.

An open limousine purred smoothly to where Hitler was seated at the edge of the tracks. With two of his generals seated in front with the helmeted chauffeur, he rode in the back of the car that carried him between columns of advancing German troops. The soldiers cheered when they saw the Fuehrer. He waved at them, smiling. A pistol was strapped to his side, a whip coiled around his wrist.

One of the generals suggested that they stop to visit a train filled with wounded German soldiers. The sight of their Fuehrer, said the general, would lift the spirits and ease the pain of the soldiers. Hitler brusquely said no. The sight of men in pain, he declared, was more than he could bear. Later that day, as his train moved slowly across the smoking and blackened Polish countryside, it passed a freight train carrying wounded Germans. The freight train stopped so Hitler's train could pass. The bandaged, gaunt soldiers stared with awe into the luxurious dining car of the Fuehrer, who was seated at a table, waiting to be served a steaming dinner. Hitler turned, saw the staring, envious eyes. Angrily he ordered the shades pulled down.

Within a week the Polish army had been smashed—from the west by Hitler's panzers, from the east by Stalin's massive army. As part of their pact, Hitler had given Stalin permission to take a huge bite out of eastern Poland.

As the Germans marched Polish soldiers in long lines toward prisoner of war camps—where many would be forced to enlist in the German army—Hitler's black-uniformed SS men, their death's-head insignia gleaming on their caps, swarmed into Poland. The new German governor of Poland announced that the "Poles shall be the slaves of the German Reich." And Hitler told his assembled generals after his return to the Chancellery in Berlin, "Our treatment of the Poles might not be to the taste of German generals, but you are not to interfere in such matters."

The SS men rounded up more than 3,000 Polish intellectuals— writers, artists, professors—and shot them. More than 1,000,000 Polish men, women, and children were forced at bayonet point out of their homes and marched to distant camps, their homes occupied by Germans who were pouring into the country as colonists. Many of those 1,000,000 Poles died that winter of 1940–41 of cold or starvation as they huddled in camps whipped by below-zero howling blizzards.

SS men strode into the homes of Jews, shot all the men in front of their horrified families, then carted out the bodies and threw them into ditches. One detachment of SS men, swinging whips, forced fifty Jews to rebuild a bridge. When the job was done, the Jews were herded into a synagogue. A machine gun was set up on a balcony. It sprayed bullets into the huddled, screaming Jews, slaughtering all.

Back in Berlin, Hitler gleefully read reports from the western front, where only a handful of German divisions were crouched behind their fortifications, facing more than 150 French and British divisions. To Hitler's delight—and his generals' amazement—the Allies had not charged into Germany, although they outnumbered the Germans six to one. After the war, Field Marshal Wilhelm Keitel said that the Allies easily could have run through "our screen" and climbed up the backs of the Germans fighting in Poland. World War II would have ended in its first seven days instead of dragging on for almost six years and consuming the lives of more than 10,000,000 men, women, and children.

The French and British had not attacked because they feared the Germans would retaliate by sending over waves of bombers to blast London and Paris. "We can no longer help Poland; it went under too quickly," they told each other and the world. "Instead, we must build up our forces to throw back the Germans when Hitler moves the bulk of his army from Poland to the west." This was hardly the aggressive war that would defeat Hitler. The war in the west soon became known as the sitzkrieg—the sit-down war.

Hitler wasn't surprised at the hesitancy of the French and British leaders—"those little worms," as he called them, whom he had bluffed for so long. Now he told the British and the French to call off their war against him. "This war in the west cannot solve any problems," he told the British and French in a soothing radio speech. "Poland will never rise again."

But Daladier and Chamberlain, with the moral, though not the political, support of President Roosevelt, informed Hitler they would not pull back their armies from the German border until Hitler withdrew from Poland. "Never!" Hitler thundered in reply. "Then you shall have war." To his cronies he said that America's Roosevelt and his own nemesis in Britain, that "whiskey-drinking fool of a Churchill," were in the pay of his archenemies the Jews.

By now Hitler's armies had swollen to more than 3,000,000, newly stocked with Poles, Austrians, Czechs, as well as teenaged Germans. Now they were numerically about the equivalent of the French and British armies facing them across the west wall—136 German divisions opposing 135 Allied divisions.

A stream of new tanks, guns, airplanes, and ammunition flowed to the German divisions from Hitler's war factories. In a blitzkrieg of their own, the German workers toiled around the clock to re-arm the army for another fierce attack. Late in September, 1939, less than a month after his plunge into Poland, Hitler assembled his generals in the Chancellery and ordered them to begin planning "for the second act of this drama"—the destruction of the Allied armies.

The generals stood around a long table in the map room of the Chancellery. Most were aging men—Field Marshal Keitel, General Halder, Field Marshal Brauchitsch—and they eyed

Hitler anxiously. A young general—his name was Fritz von Manstein—pointed to the maps with a ruler as he talked. This upstart, the older generals fumed to themselves, had caught Hitler's gaze with an outlandish and dangerous strategy to defeat the Allies.

With his ruler General Manstein pointed to an area in Belgium called the Ardennes Forest. It was thickly wooded, with many steep hills. No one in his right mind would try to drive tanks through the Ardennes; they would almost certainly stall going uphill or crash into trees coming downhill.

But General Manstein, a former tank commander, said German tanks could plow through the Ardennes, springing out at the Allied armies, which would not be expecting an armored blow from that direction.

The Manstein plan was simple. All of Germany's thousands of tanks and armored cars—the entire panzer army—would be massed in the Ardennes, the thick foliage hiding it from Allied aerial observation. Then, like a steel dagger, it would flash out of the Ardennes and race across the flat French countryside toward the English Channel. This thrust would cut the Allied armies in half. Then each half could be encircled and destroyed.

Hitler, eyes gleaming, stared at the map. He was entranced by the idea.

The older generals shook their heads. "If our tanks are bunched in the Ardennes," one said, "the other sections of our lines, without tanks, will be weak. The Allies could punch through at any point, then trap the tanks in the Ardennes and destroy them and our army."

That wouldn't happen, said General Manstein. He pointed at the map. First, he said, the Germans would smash into the tiny countries of Holland and Belgium, sitting like two eggs atop the north side of France. They were neutrals, but Manstein knew that Hitler would not hesitate to smash into a neutral country to win the war. When the Germans hit Holland and Belgium, he said, the Allies would rush troops to the north to stop the German blow.

But that blow would be only a feint, he said. As the Allies rushed to the north, the German tanks would roar out of the Ardennes to smash into the middle of the weakened Allied line.

Hitler clapped his hands. He approved the Manstein Plan (later he called the plan his own). Early in May, 1941, he gave the signal—"Danzig"—that would begin the attack on Holland and Belgium, the beginning of the Six Weeks' War, Hitler's greatest triumph.

On that morning of May 10, 1940, about 2,500 German planes filled the skies over Holland and Belgium. Bombers set aflame the Dutch city of Rotterdam. And the Dutch and Belgians stared in amazement as thousands of white dots dropped out of planes and floated down—German paratroopers, a new idea in warfare that was Hitler's own. In a few days the stunned Belgian and Dutch armies, fired at from all sides by Germans who seemed to be everywhere, had been defeated.

As Manstein had predicted, the Allied generals rushed troops to the north to stop the Germans. In the Ardennes, meanwhile, the largest array of tanks and armored cars ever assembled stood poised, a panzer army that stretched back like an iron chain for almost 100 miles into Germany. If Allied planes had spotted that line of armor, three abreast, they could have turned Hitler's Panzer army into flaming hulks and ended World War II right there. But the Allied planes were busy in dog fights with German Messerschmitts over Belgium and Holland. They never saw that column of steel.

On the sunny morning of May 14 the German tanks—with a dull loud roar heard for miles—burst out of the Ardennes, rolled over surprised Allied troops, and streaked toward the Channel.

They were led by screeching Stuka dive-bombers that scattered the French and British troops hastily thrown in the way of the juggernaut by the surprised Allies.

Racing at a speed that at first delighted and then worried Hitler, the German tanks were within a few miles of the Channel by May 20. Encircled in a giant trap were more than 500,000 French and British troops, their backs to the water and facing the muzzles of German guns.

At his headquarters in a small town on the German border Hitler worriedly demanded hourly reports from his commanders. "The French will stage a surprise counter attack to cut off our panzers," he anxiously told General Halder. "I know it." Finally he ordered the panzer units to stop.

Why? asked an incredulous Halder. In a day or two, he said, the panzers would push the Allied armies into the sea or force them to surrender. Raging and screaming, Hitler accused his generals, "You have ruined the whole operation. We are courting the danger of defeat."

Tank commanders could not believe the words when they read Hitler's orders to stop. The enemy was fleeing from them toward the Channel beaches. But obediently they stopped and watched exhausted British and French troops pause, catch their breath, then begin to dig in around the port city of Dunkirk.

In England, meanwhile, a new leader had risen to replace the now-scorned Neville Chamberlain. He was that ruddy-faced, paunchy man Hitler detested: Winston Churchill. Quickly Churchill ordered what was called Operation Dynamo. It would go down in history as the Miracle of Dunkirk.

More than 900 boats—ferryboats, tugboats, corvettes, destroyers, put-putting motorboats, even tiny sailboats—bobbed out from England and crossed the treacherous waters of the Channel, churning toward Dunkirk. Hundreds of Englishmen who had never sailed more than a mile from shore now steered their boats over the horizon to France, hoping to pluck from the beaches as many soldiers as they could carry. In handfuls at first, then by the hundreds, Allied troops swarmed off the beaches and were ferried to safety in England.

At his headquarters Hitler heard the pleas of his generals that the panzers be allowed to smash the Allied troops before they escaped. No, growled Hitler, if the panzers attacked, they might in turn be attacked from the rear by the French.

But that can't happen, his generals said.

"Anything can happen," Hitler said worriedly. Finally, however, he agreed to an idea from Goering, who was anxious that his air force share in the glory of this victory.

"The Luftwaffe will finish the job," Goering promised Hitler. "We will bomb the British and French on the beaches until nothing is left but fish bait."

Hitler's tank commanders grimaced. Later Field Marshal Gerd von Rundstedt, then a panzer commander, called Hitler's decision to stop the tanks "one of the great turning points of the war."

The Luftwaffe bombers thundered over the beaches, dropping bombs on the Allied troops cowering on the sand. But most of the bombs nosed into the sand and did not explode. And day and night boats crisscrossed the Channel, carrying more soldiers to safety in England. In a week more than a third of 1,000,000 troops had landed in England to fight again instead of being killed or taken prisoner.

Finally, Hitler, with angry stares at a red-faced Goering, gave the order for the tanks to attack. The Germans quickly captured the few remaining troops at Dunkirk and, within days, were rounding up remnants of the Allied armies. Long lines of bearded, stunned-looking French soldiers filed into the barbed-wired pens of German prisoner of war camps, where more than 1,500,000 would be caged for the next five years. Hitler's blitz had killed 136,000 French and British soldiers. The cost to the Germans had been 27,000 dead.

On the morning of June 17 Hitler stood at a long table, studying maps inside his headquarters, which was called Wolf's Gorge. His staff had occupied all the houses in a small Belgian village, its inhabitants forced onto roads at bayonet point and ordered not to return.

Hitler smiled happily as his generals pointed on the maps to the collapsing French lines. German armies were slicing through all of France. And in the south of France the French had been attacked by the Italians. Emboldened by Hitler's success and anxious to share in the booty of war, Mussolini had joined his Axis partner at last, pouncing upon the shattered French army. President Roosevelt angrily called Mussolini's lunge at a defeated France "a stab in the back."

As Hitler studied the maps, a messenger arrived. He carried a note that was handed to Hitler. The French had asked for an armistice. They wanted to discuss surrender.

Hitler slapped one hand against his thigh. His knee jerked upward. "He was literally shaken by frantic exuberance," one of his secretaries later said. The fawning General Keitel seemed to bow over Hitler's boots as he shouted, "My Fuehrer, you are the greatest generalissimo of all time!"

Hitler had already decided where he would accept the French surrender: in a little clearing of a forest near Compiègne, a small French town. Some 32 years earlier, in that same clearing near Compiègne, the German people had been forced to accept their greatest humiliation. Seated in a railway dining car, German emissaries had signed the armistice that had ended World War I with Germany defeated and soon to be harnessed by the reins of the Treaty of Versailles.

Now Hitler wrote his reply to the French request for an armistice. The French generals, he said, would have to meet him at that same railway car in the forest near Compiègne.

On June 21st—almost six weeks after the start of his blitzkreig—Hitler drove in the front seat of his black Mercedes through the thick forest. The day was warm, the sun bright, and birds chirped in the foliage. Arriving at the clearing, which had become a French historical museum, Hitler stepped from his car. He strode toward a high stone monument, walked onto it, and read the inscription.

HERE ON THE ELEVENTH DAY OF NOVEMBER 1918 SUCCUMBED THE CRIMINAL PRIDE OF THE GERMAN EMPIRE—VANQUISHED BY THE FREE PEOPLES WHICH IT TRIED TO ENSLAVE.

Watching Hitler's face was American war correspondent William L. Shirer. In his diary Shirer wrote: "I have seen that face many times at the great moments of his life. But today! It is afire with scorn, anger, hate, revenge, triumph. He steps off the monument and contrives to make even this gesture a masterpiece of contempt. He glances back at it, contemptuous, angry—angry, you almost feel, because he cannot wipe out the awful, provoking letters with one sweep of his high Prussian boot. . ."

Hitler, followed by a chain of generals, entered the railway dining car, which had been preserved by the French as the prize spectacle of this museum. The French generals arrived, their faces somber as they realized what was about to happen in this place revered in French history and hearts.

General Keitel read the German terms for a cease-fire that would end France's agony—terms a French general later called "merciless." When Keitel finished reading, Hitler stood and stalked out. His message was clear to the French: Accept my terms or none!

The French reluctantly signed. To encourage French men and women to pour labor and material into his war machine, Hitler set up a "new and free France."

A zone not occupied by German soldiers was carved out of the south of France. The capital of unoccupied France was Vichy. Head of the "Vichy regime," as the newest Hitler puppet government was called, was the aged and doddering Marshal Henri Pétain, a World War I hero (after the war Petain and other French "collaborators" as they were called, stood trial for treason).

Hitler, after striding out of the railway car, again passed the French monument to the November 11, 1918, armistice. Three days later, at Hitler's order, it was blown up.

He set off on a sightseeing tour of Paris, that "city of light" that had always fascinated the artist in him. He stood, cap over his heart, at the tomb of Napoleon, the French conqueror of a century earlier. After a long silence Hitler turned to an aide and ordered that plans be started for building his tomb. It would be in Munich, he said. "Here I was truly born, here I started my movement, and here is my heart."

In his open Mercedes Hitler toured the narrow, cobbled streets of Montmartre, that hilly area of Paris where artists dwell. As the car rolled by a market-place, a woman recognized him and shouted, "It's him! It's him!" And from a house another shrieked, "The devil!" and slammed down her window. Amused, Hitler watched the women scatter and run.

That night he slept in Paris as the master of nearly all of Europe, for he had captured Denmark and Norway with lightning assaults earlier that spring. His swastika floated from the English Channel to the Bug River on the rim of Russia, and from near the Arctic Circle to the sunny shores of the French Riviera.

Across the Atlantic Americans had gaped with astonishment at black headlines telling of the sudden fall of France, that proud nation whose army—Americans had thought only a few weeks earlier—was the best in the world. "The future belongs to Hitler," crowed one admiring American writer. "It seems as though nothing or no one can stop him."

In London's historic House of Commons chamber, however, the rotund, pink-jowled Winston Churchill, England's new leader, rose to shout words that rang with defiance, and his speech would go down as among the most inspiring of all time. England would go on fighting, he told a world listening by radio. ". . .we shall defend our island, whatever the cost may be. We shall fight on the beaches, we shall fight on the landing grounds, we shall fight in the fields, and in the streets, we shall fight in the hills. . ."

And then, slowly and emphatically, he told the cheering members of the House of Commons, "We shall never surrender!"

Hitler, face aglow with triumph, inspected the Channel beaches. He saw litter stretching for miles—the guns, boots, helmets, and packs left by a routed army. He tried to brush aside his failure to destroy the British army. "It is always good," he told his generals, "to let a broken army return home to show the civilian population what a beating they have had."

England now stood alone against Hitler's mailed fist. The little island nation could be ringed by submarines, their torpedoes blowing cargo vessels out of the water and starving the English into surrender. Or England could be bombed by the Luftwaffe into a smoking ash heap. Or the German armies, poised on the coast of France only a few miles from England's white cliffs, could try to sail across the treacherous Channel and swarm over an army stripped of most of its guns, ammunition and more than a little of its swagger.

Hitler was confident the British would beg for peace. He

wanted peace with England. Then England and the United States would have to stand and watch while he turned toward the east to conquer Russia.

Hitler began to march his troops eastward toward Russia. Behind the Kremlin walls in Moscow the usually shrewd Stalin, lulled by Hitler's treaty of friendship, could not believe that Hitler would attack.

Hitler, an avid reader of history books, knew well their lessons: that Kaiser Wilhelm's World War I army had worn itself out fighting the Russians in the east and the Allies in the west; and that Napoleon, the greatest conqueror until Hitler, had been defeated by Russia's vastness and bitter winter, his retreating troops blooded and slaughtered on Russia's snow-covered steppes.

By that time, however, Hitler had become fatally infected by a sin the ancient Greeks called "hubris"—overwhelming pride. No nation, army, or general could stop him, "the greatest generalissimo of all time." However, a wraith was forming on the horizon behind the seemingly endless Russian plains, a wraith that would form into an icy-white giant named General Winter, and that General Winter would be the first to stop Hitler.

16

"A Flight from the Snow"

Waving a piece of paper in his hand, Hitler burst into the conference room in the Chancellery. Two of his generals, seated at a long table, turned to stare. One later said, "This was the wildest rage I had ever seen him go through."

"This is a personal insult to me!" he screeched, slapping a hand at the paper, which the generals saw was a telegram. "Now all our plans for Operation Barbarossa are in peril. But I will show the Yugoslavians. . . .The blow against Yugoslavia will be carried out with merciless harshness and the military destruction will be done in blitzkrieg style." And he added ominously, "Now I intend to make a clean sweep of the Balkans. It is time people got to know me better."

Hitler ordered Goering to send over waves of Luftwaffe bombers to "smash Yugoslavia militarily and as a state." He named the assault Operation Punishment—he would teach the Yugoslavians a lesson they would never forget.

He was also making what was probably the biggest blunder of his life. To teach the Yugoslavians a lesson by hammering them with Operation Punishment, Hitler—on this dark afternoon of March 27, 1941—was postponing Operation Barbarossa—his attack on Russia—for at least four weeks. In *The Rise and Fall of the Third Reich,* historian William L. Shirer wrote:

This postponement of the attack on Russia in order that the Nazi warlord might vent his personal spite against a small Balkan country which had dared to defy him was probably the most catastrophic single decision in Hitler's career. It is hardly too much to say that by making it that March afternoon in the Chancellery in Berlin, during a moment of convulsive rage, he tossed away his last golden opportunity to win the war and to make . . . himself the master of Europe.

On that fateful March morning Hitler had awakened early, as usual, in his plainly furnished bedroom in the Chancellery. ("I feel most comfortable in a simple ordinary bed," he often said.) In a nearby bedroom slept Eva Braun, a willowy and blond former photographer's assistant who had become Hitler's mistress. Her chauffeur once called Eva Braun "the loneliest woman in Germany." She often weepingly told friends that although she loved Hitler, he did not love her. When the wives of Goering or Goebbels visited the Chancellery for parties, Eva had to sit alone in her room. Hitler wanted her to be seen as seldom as possible, since although he was living with her, she was not his wife.

Eva desperately wanted Hitler to marry her. But he brusquely told her, sometimes in front of other people, that he was too busy as a warlord to be a husband. A woman who spent hours looking at herself in the mirror and talking with girlfriends about fashions and the latest movies, Eva knew little about politics. When Hitler left by train for the war fronts, she sat in her small bedroom in the Chancellery or at the Eagle's Nest, alone, without letters from him, torturing herself by imagining he would one day

MAD DICTATOR OF WORLD WAR II

throw her out and marry someone else. Hitler seemed to have cared for Eva, the way a child might care for a pretty kitten, but —with the possible exception of Geli—he seemed incapable of having a full and loving affair with any woman.

He now pored over war maps for hours on end. He left the running of Germany to others, more and more to the stocky, sinister Martin Bormann, his secretary. Bormann often suggested a decision that Hitler then approved. To the anger and jealousy of Goebbels, Goering, and Himmler, the crafty, tough Bormann had become Germany's number two ruler. His rivals called him "the man who secretly ran Germany."

It was almost a year since Hitler had smashed the Allies in the Six Weeks' War. On this day in March, 1941, his African forces under General Erwin Rommel—the Desert Fox—were poised to storm across the wastes of North Africa toward the Suez Canal. If they could achieve a victory, it might make Hitler the master of the Mediterranean.

Meanwhile Hitler had watched, enraged, as England withstood waves of bombardment by Goering's Luftwaffe. Young English pilots, some only teenagers, rose in their fast Spitfires to shoot down the slow-moving German Junkers. Hitler didn't know—nor would most people until almost thirty years after the war—that Churchill and the British had broken some of the important German codes and therefore had advance knowledge of enemy moves. This was about the only advantage enjoyed by the small, battered British army over the German army and its reluctant allies, totalling more than 4,000,000 troops. By that time Mussolini had screwed up his courage and put his inferior forces behind Hitler. Other allies of Germany were Hungary, Rumania, Bulgaria, and Finland. On this March day in 1941 Hitler had moved about 3,000,000 German and "foreign" troops onto a 900-mile line facing Russia.

Leaving his bedroom on this March morning, Hitler walked down a hallway to a conference room, where Halder, Brauchitsch, and Goering waited to confer with him over the war maps. "His face was drawn and haggard," an American war correspondent had written a few days earlier. "His skin was ashy gray, his eyes devoid of their usual luster. Care and worry was [sic] stamped on him."

For despite victory after victory, Hitler was haunted by a gnawing fear that he would fail and be destroyed. "If we fail," he told the German people in a radio speech, "we will have no choice: We will be annihiliated. Ahead is only annihilation of others or being annihilated ourselves!"

With his generals Hitler studied war maps posted on the walls of the conference room. Before Operation Barbarossa could be launched against Russia—the date was set for May 1, only a month hence—Hitler wanted to occupy Greece. His reason seemed almost childlike: Mussolini had been soundly buffeted when the Italians had attacked Greece a few months earlier. That defeat, he told his generals, "struck a blow at the belief of our invincibility." He wanted to smash the Greeks to remind the world that no one could stop him.

The road to Greece ran through Hungary, Rumania, and Bulgaria, where German troops were now massed. But Yugoslavia, a Balkan neighbor of Greece's, had refused to join Hitler as an ally—and the crack Yugoslavian army, Hitler feared, might sideswipe his army when it invaded Greece.

Hitler threatened and cajoled Yugoslavia during March, 1941. Finally, its ruler, Prince Paul, agreed to align his country with Germany against Greece. Hitler was overjoyed. All his patience had been expended lining up the Yugoslavs so he could wipe out Greece and turn on May 1 to his prime target: Russia.

Then, suddenly on that morning of March 27, came the telegram that enraged him. Prince Paul had been overthrown by Yugoslavs who were angered by the alliance with Hitler. A band of young military officers had seized power and told the world that they would oppose any German thrust into the Balkans.

At first Hitler couldn't believe the words of the telegram. Then he began to rage, vowing his "clean sweep of the Balkans"— Operation Punishment against Yugoslavia.

Within hours German bombers droned over Belgrade, the Yugoslavian capital. They dropped bombs on the defenseless city, killing 17,000 men, women, and children. The German armies surged over the outnumbered Yugoslavian troops and within two weeks had destroyed or captured most of them. And by late April the huge German force had blasted into Greece and captured the ancient capital Athens. But, as John Toland wrote in *Adolf Hitler,* "a sledgehammer had been used to kill mosquitoes." Hitler had used far more troops and planes than he had needed to crush the Yugoslavs and Greeks. And he had taken those troops and planes from where they had been massed on the border facing Russia. He was forced to postpone the attack on Russia while troops, tanks, and planes were rerouted laboriously back to the Russian border—a seven-week delay that would be fatal.

Hitler set a new date, June 22, for Operation Barbarossa. In an address to his generals, he told them what he had told the German people in the 1920's: that only he could stop the "staining" spread of "Jewish-Russian bolshevism" over the globe.

At times Hitler seemed confident that victory over Russia would be easy. "Once we kick in the door," he told his generals, "the whole rotten house will fall down." But at other times he seemed frightened: "I feel as if I am pushing open the door to a dark room. One can never know what lies beyond the door."

He was well aware that Germany had been crushed by fighting

a two-front war in 1914–18—against Russia in the east and the Allies in the west. "I had always maintained that we ought at all costs to avoid waging war on two fronts," he later told Bormann, "and you may rest assured that I pondered long and anxiously over Napoleon and his experiences in Russia. But there was no hope of ending the war by invasion of England, and hostilities would have gone on interminably."

Hitler was now cocking an anxious eye at the United States, which was supplying Britain with food, ammunition, tanks, and guns. Hitler knew that his ally in the Pacific, Japan, was preparing for war. If Japan and America began to shoot at each other, Hitler reasoned, America would line up with England against the three Axis Powers—Germany, Japan, and Italy. The industrial might of America, he decided, could be matched only if Germany held the richness of Russia—its millions of square miles of grain and oil. Then the German empire, with the Japanese keeping the Americans occupied in the Pacific, would be at least as strong as, and perhaps stronger than, the industrial might of the United States.

In the days before June 22 Britain's code breakers unearthed Hitler's plan to attack the Russians. The British warned Stalin of an imminent, massive attack. But Stalin, suspicious that Churchill wanted to draw him into the war against Hitler, paid no heed. On the morning of June 22, as a rosy dawn spread over the Bug River, which separated German and Russian troops in Poland, German guns belched fire, dropping shells into the Russian lines. The Russian soldiers were astounded. One general radioed Moscow: "We are being fired upon. What shall we do?"

Moscow radioed back: "You must be insane."

Some 3,000,000 German, Hungarian, Bulgarian, and Italian troops steamrollered over the stunned Russians. Racing as fast as 200 miles a day, the German tanks and armored cars streaked toward Moscow. A delighted Hitler told Germans, listening on radio, that "the enemy in the east has been struck down and will never rise again." And he boasted that his troops, in only a few weeks, had seized Russian territory "twice the size of the German Reich when I came to power in 1933."

On and on the German army rolled, the Russians scattering before them. But the countryside seemed to stretch toward an unreachable horizon. Russia appeared to go on forever.

German generals began to worry. They had expected to face 200 Russian divisions. By September they had counted 360. "When we destroy a dozen Russian divisions," a general reported to Hitler, "the Russians reach back and throw in twelve fresh divisions."

Other German generals looked anxiously at the darkening autumn skies. Their troops were shivering in their summer uniforms. The German army had not brought winter overcoats or boots. Operation Barbarossa had been calculated as a four-month campaign that would have ended, if it had begun on May 1, on September 1, well before the start of the fierce Russian winter. But Operation Punishment had pushed back the starting date six weeks to June 22. Now the Germans had to vanquish the Russians in four months—by October 22—or face the ordeal of fighting in their light clothes amid freezing blizzards.

The panzer spearheads began to slow as they closed to within 100 miles of Moscow, where Stalin nervously paced behind the ancient walls of the Kremlin. Columns of German troops were harassed by Russian snipers, who fired, killed, then vanished into the expanse of countryside. The October 22 deadline passed, and as the Germans slogged on, their faces were buffeted by icy winds. Temperatures dipped to ten degrees above zero. The Germans huddled together at night for warmth. In the mornings fires had to be lit under tanks to warm up their engines.

183

Then came heavy, blinding snow. One German commander later wrote of "the endless expanse of Russian snow . . . swirling snow buried fallen soldiers, hit by sniper fire, and within minutes they had disappeared under a blanket of white. Hour after hour the infantry slogged behind tanks, one painful step at a time through the thickening snow, dressed in thin summer uniforms, while all around them, fur-clad Russian troops, dashing across the snow on snowshoes, fired, killed, then ran."

At his warm headquarters on the Russian border—he called it Wolf's Lair—Hitler sent orders to his commanders to capture Moscow, where his army would find warmth; from Moscow they could conquer the rest of Russia in the spring. "One final heave," he radioed his troops, "and we shall triumph."

On the morning of December 3 he clapped his hands gleefully when told that German scouts had ridden on motorcycles into a suburb of Moscow. With their binoculars the scouts could see the towers of the Kremlin. But the next day the scouts were driven out of the suburb by a band of factory workers firing rifles.

Hitler's army would never get closer to Moscow.

Out of the snow and howling winds burst a line of Russians, 100 miles wide. It smashed into the German army and sent it reeling. At first the Germans retreated slowly, firing as they fell back, and then they began to throw away their guns and run.

At Wolf's Lair Hitler read reports of one German division after another vanishing under the Russian onslaught. He ordered death for any soldier who ran. He sulked, refusing to eat with his generals, blaming them for this defeat. One by one he began to fire his generals. That onetime plotter, General Halder, was among the first to go. General Keitel, now the commander in chief, was terrified that he would be executed. Whatever Hitler said, Keitel shouted, "Yes, my Fuehrer," and immediately dashed out of the room to make sure the orders—however frantic or unwise—were obeyed.

Amazingly, in that far-off frozen expanse, Hitler's soldiers obeyed his hysterical orders to stop and fight. Divisions coiled into circles and fought off the Russians just as the western pioneers, barricaded behind a circle of covered wagons, had shot at Indians.

"It was Hitler's one great achievement," a general said after the war. "If the troops had begun a retreat, it might have turned into a panic flight."

But the isolated German divisions were mauled by the circling Russians. Before the winter storms faded into the rains of spring, about 300,000 of Hitler's soldiers had been killed or wounded, or were missing. More than 100,000 others were crippled by frostbite; blackened arms and legs often had to be amputated.

The sullen Hitler, now keeping more and more to himself (his most-frequent companion was his wolfhound, Blondi), decided to leave Wolf's Lair. He went back to Berchtesgaden. He was met at his Eagle's Nest retreat by the thin-faced Goebbels. Hitler walked into his spacious office and stared out through the giant window at the Alps, which were covered with a line of white snow.

Hitler spun, his face crimson with fury, and stalked out of the room. The next day he flew in his Junker to Berlin. Goebbels said to one of his assistants as they flew away from the Eagle's Nest. "It's a kind of flight from the snow."

That snow—the killing weapon of General Winter—had inflicted on the warlord his first military defeat. Another awaited him at a place called Stalingrad.

17

"I Know the Americans"

"Is this report correct?" Hitler shouted, a smile appearing on his pale, sharp face.

"Yes, my Fuehrer," snapped the officer who had just handed him the typewritten sheet of paper. Hitler scanned it again, sitting at his desk at Wolf's Lair, where he had been getting reports on the German drive toward Moscow. The date was December 7, 1941.

The message just handed him was a report from Tokyo that Japanese warplanes had bombed Pearl Harbor, the American naval base in the Pacific. Now Japan had joined Germany and Italy.

"We cannot lose the war!" Hitler laughed, putting down the report. "Now we have a partner who has not been defeated in three thousand years."

Hitler's generals told him they feared the might of a growing American army and the millions of guns, tanks, planes, and ships that would now flow from America's factories.

"From my days at the front," Hitler scoffed, "I know the Americans. They will run when they see comrades fall around them. And as for their factories, we will soon control all Russia, filled with natural resources that will last Germany for a thousand years. With Russia's oil and grain, we can equal the production of the United States, which must send half of its troops and war matériel to the Pacific. Within a few months after we conquer Russia, I assure you, the American and British will be brought to the point of discussing peace."

As a sunny spring of 1942 warmed his troops in Russia, Hitler's mind was fixed on two objectives. One was to capture Moscow, the political heart of Russia. The second was to capture the oil and grain fields of southern Russia. The gateway to those fields, he told his generals, was the city of Stalingrad. "If we don't get those fields," he told his generals, now in one of his dark moods, "I will have to end the war."

One afternoon, as Hitler sat over maps in the sweltering barrackslike building that was his headquarters, a young general began to protest that Hitler was asking too much of his army. "We should concentrate on Moscow or the Caucasus," he said. "Not both."

"I expect my commanders to be as tough as my fighting troops," Hitler snarled, eyes gleaming.

Hesitantly, the general replied that thousands of German soldiers had died because of Hitler's decisions so far in this Russian campaign.

"How dare you use language like that in front of me?" Hitler shouted, standing "Do you think you can teach me what the man at the front is thinking? What do you know what goes on at the front? Where were you in the First World War? And you try to present to me that I don't understand what it's like at the front? It's outrageous."

Yet, as fiercely as Hitler could lash his generals, he spoke gently to his secretaries, valets, chauffeurs, and other "little people" around him. He often told them how, as a starving artist in Munich and Vienna thirty years before, he had been humiliated by bosses and "haughty upper-class people." He told how he and other starving men had shoveled snow to open the way through drifts so rich society ladies and gentlemen could enter the lobby of an opera—and how they had stalked by him and his fellow workers without even a "thank you, as though we didn't exist."

Hitler seemed to identify himself with the people who worked for him—he could easily be one of them. When a nervous secretary's hand shook as she jotted down his dictation, he told her, "Don't worry, I will make more mistakes in my grammar than you will make in writing down what I say."

At his headquarters he seemed to prefer the companionship of secretaries and gardeners, as well as his wolfhound, to that of his generals, whose hands he refused to shake at their morning meetings. He even seemed strained and aloof from old cronies like Goebbels, whenever he flew from Berlin to Wolf's Lair. "His dog," Goebbels said sadly after one visit, "seems to be his best friend."

Back in Berlin high Nazi officials began to whisper that the Fuehrer had gone mad. One doctor told of visiting Hitler and hearing him mutter, "I must go to India, I must. . . ." And another told of hearing Hitler shout hysterically, "For one German who is killed, ten of the enemy must die, must die, must die. . . ."

Millions of innocent noncombatants would die in this war at Hitler's order. By now Hitler's SS extermination squads had rounded up more than 300,000 Jews in Russia. Some were shipped to killing centers like Treblinka in Poland. Others were marched out of villages, ordered to dig ditches, then cut down by machine gunners. After the war a German engineer described what he had seen on a road outside a town in Russia:

The people who had got off the truck—men, women, and children of all ages—had to undress upon the order of an SS man, who carried a riding or dog whip. . . . Without scream-ing or weeping, these people undressed, stood around in family groups, kissed each other, said farewell.

. . . an old woman with snow-white hair was holding a one-year-old child in her arms and singing to it. . . . The parents were looking on with tears in their eyes. The father was hold-ing the hand of a boy about ten years old and speaking to him softly; the boy was fighting back his tears. The father pointed to the sky, stroked his head, and seemed to explain something to him. . . .

. . .I walked around the mound and found myself con-fronted by a tremendous grave. People were closely wedged together and lying on top of each other so that only their heads were visible. Nearly all had blood running from their shoulders, from their heads. . . . Some were lifting their arms and turning their heads to show they were still alive. The pit was already two-thirds full. I estimated that it contained about a thousand people. I looked for the man who did the shooting. He was an SS man who sat at the edge of the nar-row end of the pit. . . . He had a tommy gun on his knees and was smoking a cigarette.

The people, completely naked, went down some steps and clambered over the heads of people lying there. . . . They lay down in front of dead or wounded people. . . . Then I heard a series of shots. I looked into the pit and saw that the bodies were twitching or heads were lying already motionless on top of the bodies that lay beneath them. . . . The next batch [of

190

victims] was approaching already. They went down into the pit, lined themselves up against the previous victims, and were shot. . . .

In the fall of 1942 Hitler's Sixth Army, commanded by General Friedrich von Paulus, stormed into Stalingrad, the key to the Caucasus. By that time other German armies had thrust eastward toward the gateway cities of Asia. In the west they occupied most of western Europe. To the south, in Africa, Hitler's "Desert Fox," General Erwin Rommel, had swept the English almost into the Red Sea. The German Reich now enslaved more than 250,000,000 people in an area slightly larger than the size of the continental United States.

Hitler's fleet of submarines prowled the North Atlantic, streaking torpedoes at convoys of merchant ships struggling toward Britain and Russia with badly needed ammunition, guns, and tanks from American factories. For a while it seemed the Atlantic was Hitler's ocean, some of the Nazi U-boats so daring that they sneaked along the east coast of the United States. Dozens of American ships were torpedoed only a few miles from Boston, New York, Philadelphia, Baltimore, and Miami Beach.

Hitler was now the master of almost half the globe. And he had already drawn up plans for what he would do when he conquered the other side of the globe—the North American continent. In a secret memo he described in chilling terms what he would do after the Americans had capitulated and his Nazi swastika floated over Washington, D.C.

"The most important part of final victory," he wrote, "will be the exclusion of the United States from world politics for all time and the destruction of their Jewish community. For this purpose Dr. Goebbels will have dictatorial authority as governor [of the United States] to accomplish the total reeducation of the racially mixed and inferior population. Goering will help in this respect, above all by mobilizing all those with German blood, at least fifty percent of the inhabitants, so they can be educated militarily and regenerated nationalistically."

Hitler's Sixth Army captured Stalingrad early in November, then stalled as it tried to battle through the Russians toward the Caucasian fields. The German generals heard rumors of a giant buildup by the Russian forces around Stalingrad. But they were reluctant to tell Hitler. Sneering, he had repeatedly accused them of "overestimating the enemy" and chided them for being "afraid of shadows."

Suddenly, at dawn on November 19, German and Rumanian troops at Stalingrad saw a tidal wave of brown Russian uniforms loom out of the darkness, led by tanks and armored cars spitting fire. Before nightfall, more than 500,000 Russians had swept over the Germans from the west. At the same time another Russian army lunged at the Germans from the east. The two armies joined, locking in an iron circle more than 250,000 of Hitler's Sixth Army.

Immediately General Paulus ordered his divisions to mass their strength for a push to the southwest sector of the circle, retreating from Stalingrad. But Hitler radioed orders not to retreat. Help, he assured Paulus, would be coming.

Two armored divisions began to drive toward the encircled Sixth Army. Hitler ordered the divisions to ram their way through the Russian circle and join the Sixth Army.

Hitler's top generals at Wolf's Lair couldn't believe what they read when they saw his orders. They protested to Hitler: Didn't he want the two armored divisions to pry open the trap for a few days so the Sixth Army could squeeze through and retreat to safety?

No! shouted Hitler. He would never leave Stalingrad. Perhaps it was because of the city's name, perhaps because it was the entry to the riches he needed, but he would not let Stalingrad out of his grasp.

The Russians stopped the armored divisions before they could get to Stalingrad. Inside the city the trapped Sixth Army soldiers huddled in cellars and smashed buildings as the Russians drew tighter the circle around them.

"Conditions are desperate here," Paulus radioed to Hitler. "Wounded freeze to death where they fall. There is no medicine. Many men have not eaten for days." He asked permission to surrender. Never, replied Hitler. The Sixth Army, he ordered, "must fight to the last man."

Only a few light planes could land in the city, bringing in messages, taking out a few lucky wounded. Among the wounded German soldiers in Stalingrad was Leo Raubal, the brother of the tragic Geli and Hitler's nephew. The Fuehrer was told that his nephew could be flown out. Hitler said his nephew should stay; he should receive no special favors.

Week by week through winter blizzards the Russians cut savagely into the shrinking circle of German defenders. Dead German bodies littered every street. The Russians cut the German force in half, then pleaded with Paulus to surrender his freezing, starved, and exhausted troops. Near Christmas Eve Paulus radioed Hitler: "Troops without ammunition or food. . . . 18,000 wounded without any supplies or dressings or drugs. . . . Further defense senseless. Army requests immediate permission to surrender in order to save lives of remaining troops."

"Surrender is forbidden," Hitler replied. "Sixth Army will hold their position to the last man . . . to the last round."

On through December and all through January the Sixth Army grimly held on. Of the 285,000 troops who had stormed into the city, fewer than 100,000 were still alive. Most of those fought with dirty, bloody bandages covering wounds and with legs and arms blackened by frostbite.

On January 30, 1943, after three months of siege, General Paulus—with Russian troops hammering at the door of his head-quarters in a cellar—sent a last message: "The Sixth Army . . . have held their position to the last man . . . the last round for the Fuehrer and fatherland until the end."

The Russians rounded up 91,000 dazed, frozen German and Rumanian soldiers, the survivors of the 285,000 who had taken this city three months earlier. Of the 91,000 who were marched off to Stalin's brutal prisoner of war camps, only 5,000 returned to Germany some dozen years later. Among those lucky ones who did return home was Leo Raubal.

In Germany Hitler proclaimed four days of national mourning after the defeat at Stalingrad. All theaters and movie houses were closed. An angry Hitler cursed Paulus and said he should have shot himself rather than permitted himself to be captured. "How easy to do that," he said, "a revolver makes it easy. What cowardice to be afraid of that."

Stalingrad had been Hitler's greatest defeat. Now his armies would begin to fall back toward Germany on every side. And in Germany a few men told each other that Hitler was pulling the German people toward a pit of flame. They began to plot to kill him.

18

"Nothing Is Fated to Happen to Me"

The tall, one-armed German colonel strode into the small room. He was carrying a heavy briefcase in his left hand. The windows of the barrackslike building here at Wolf's Lair, on the Russian-German border, had been thrown open on this hot July day. Hitler was seated at the end of a long table. Standing and facing Hitler was a general, who was showing the Fuehrer, with a pointer, where the enemy had jabbed open a hole in the Nazi lines in Russia.

General Keitel, the docile head of Hitler's General Staff, had walked into the room with the colonel. "My Fuehrer," Keitel said loudly (for Hitler had become slightly deaf), "Colonel Stauffenberg is here to present his report on the home front troops."

Hitler glanced upward from the maps. He stared at Keitel and Klaus Schenk von Stauffenberg. "First I will hear this report on the Russian front," he snapped. "Then I will hear Stauffenberg's."

Meekly General Keitel saluted. Colonel Stauffenberg put down his briefcase, pushing it under the table where Hitler sat. The briefcase, its sides bulging, rested six feet from the dictator's feet.

Colonel Stauffenberg looked at the watch on his left wrist. He had lost his right arm and one eye as a tank commander in Africa and now commanded the home troops, which patrolled German cities to guard against an invasion by paratroopers. The time was 12:37 in the early afternoon of July 20, 1944. There were no sounds except for the general's voice droning through the humid heat. Several other officers bent their heads over the maps.

Colonel Stauffenberg tapped the elbow of an officer near him. "I must go and telephone," Stauffenberg said. "Keep an eye on my briefcase. It has secret papers in it."

The officer nodded. Stauffenberg walked quickly out of the room, strode down a corridor and through the door of the low and flat wooden building. A few hundred feet away, he looked again at his watch. The time was 12:38. There were four minutes left, he realized, before that briefcase at Hitler's feet would explode. It contained a bomb that Stauffenberg and his fellow conspirators believed was powerful enough to kill Hitler.

Several times since 1938 Hitler had come within a few minutes or a few feet from a bomb that would have killed him and ended the war. In 1939 he had spoken at a beer hall in Munich while a bomb, planted by a German workman, sat with its fuse burning only a few feet away. But Hitler, anxious to catch a train to go to the Polish front, wound up his speech earlier than expected, and instead of chatting with old comrades, as he usually did, he dashed from the hall. Minutes later the bomb exploded, killing seven people who stood near where Hitler had been standing. "The fact that I left the Bürgenbräukeller earlier than usual," cried Hitler when he heard of the bombing, "is proof of Providence's intention to let me reach my goal!"

By July, 1944, most of Hitler's generals and even Goebbels and Goering knew that the war was lost. Thousands of American and British bombers droned daily over Germany, dropping bombs that turned cities into huge bonfires. In one "carpet bombing" of the city of Hamburg, 70,000 people were killed. Factories were blown up. German industrialists told Hitler that they could no longer turn out guns, planes, and tanks if the bombings went on pounding their factories into flaming heaps.

Before the war Goering had breezily assured Hitler, "No enemy plane will ever enter Germany." Now a quivering drug addict who steered his mind away from the war's disasters by playing with toy trains, Goering visited Hamburg in late 1943, then broke down and wept. Goebbels stared at the wrecked city, turned to an aide, and said, "What if we lose?" He began to carry a pistol.

While German cities burned in 1943 and 1944, Hitler's troops were being pushed back toward the inferno. In the west a giant Allied army, composed of American, Canadian, British, and French troops and commanded by General Dwight D. Eisenhower, had crossed the Channel and landed in France on June 6, 1944. Allied tanks were now clanking down dusty French roads toward Germany. In the east Stalin's army was pushing Hitler's battered invaders out of Russia, leaving behind more than 1,000,000 German dead. And from the south another Allied army, having swept the Germans out of Africa, was now thrusting up through Italy.

His toadying top general, Keitel, kept reassuring Hitler. "How many difficult situations we have already survived!" he told Hitler. "We shall survive this one, too, my Fuehrer!"

Hitler himself, besieged by reports from his generals that teenage boys and fifty-year-old men would have to be drafted to replenish the thinning army or from his industrialists that the German war machine was breaking down, would rise from his seat and roar, "We have survived worse crises than this! We will survive this!"

But one crisis after another, especially since the defeat at

Stalingrad in 1942, had aged him these past two years. German doctors later said that Hitler aged four years during each twelve months of the last years of the war. He swallowed drugs to quiet his torn nerves. The entire right side of his body shook uncontrollably, and he had to grip his right hand with his left hand to keep it from shaking wildly. He walked at a stooped, shuffling gait. At his Wolf's Lair headquarters, said Goebbels, "he no longer goes out in the fresh air, no longer has any relaxation. He sits in his bunker and broods." And following the defeats in Russia, a general noted that Hitler, after losing his temper, "was then unpredictable in what he said and decided."

Yet he was still the fatherlike figure to his secretaries—but a dull one. "After Stalingrad," recalled one of them, "Hitler would not listen to music anymore, and every evening we had to listen to his monologues instead. . . . It was always the same: his early days in Vienna, his struggles, the history of man, the microcosm and the macrocosm. On every subject we knew in advance what he would say. In the course of time these monologues bored us. But world affairs and events at the front were never mentioned; everything to do with the war was taboo."

His generals and secretaries often nodded, fighting sleep, as Hitler droned on. Then, when he and Eva Braun went to bed, the staff danced and drank cognac until dawn, light-spirited now that his dark presence was no longer among them.

As the German generals rode with their troops out of Russia, they passed huge mounds. These were the mass graves where thousands of slaughtered Jews, Gypsies, Poles, and other "Slavic subhumans" had been buried. SS squads poured gasoline on those mounds and set them aflame to destroy the evidence of their wholesale murders. Other generals learned to their horror how almost 500,000 Jews had been led into chambers to be poisoned—

hundreds at a time—by gas fumes. This was the climax of what Hitler had promised: his "final solution" to what Goebbels called "the life-and-death struggle between the Aryan race and the Jewish bacillus."

The generals, now distraught as they saw Germany being crushed between two approaching armies, decided to kill Hitler, then ask President Roosevelt and Prime Minister Churchill for peace. They hoped to keep on fighting the Russians. They feared that Stalin, made bloodthirsty by Hitler's double cross and his savagery in Russia, would put a torch to German cities and enslave the German people.

As part of that conspiracy, Colonel Stauffenberg had come to Hitler's Wolf's Lair headquarters in Prussia and planted his bomb at Hitler's feet. The time was now 12:40—two minutes to explosion.

Inside the humid room the officer's voice droned on as flies buzzed around his sweaty face. Hitler stared with lusterless eyes at the maps spread in front of him.

Another officer leaned over to peer at the maps. His foot struck Stauffenberg's brief case. He tried to toe it aside. But the heavy briefcase did not budge. The officer reached down, picked up the briefcase and placed it on the other side of a heavy wooden block that supported the table. That wooden block was now a barrier between Hitler's legs and the bomb.

Outside, standing in the baking sun, Stauffenberg looked anxiously at his watch. The time was 12:42. The bomb should go off at any second.

Inside the room the general was finishing. "If our army group around Lake Peipus is not immediately withdrawn, a catastrophe—"

With the roar of 100 trucks exploding into life, the bomb went off. A tongue of fire leaped out of the building, followed by a mushrooming cloud of black smoke. Stauffenberg saw legs, arms, and bodies hurtle through the air as debris splattered onto the ground around him.

No one could have lived through that blast, he told himself. "It was just like a direct hit by a 155-millimeter shell," he later told his fellow conspirators. But he made the mistake of rushing away from the headquarters before he was certain that Hitler was dead.

He flew back to Berlin. He landed, expecting to be informed that Goebbels and Goering had been arrested and that troops, loyal to the plotting generals, had seized government offices.

To his amazement, driving through Berlin, Stauffenberg saw that nothing had happened. The generals had been afraid to order the troops to arrest Goebbels and Goering in their dread that Hitler might still be alive.

Stauffenberg assured the generals that Hitler was dead. Finally, the generals acted. They ordered a major to arrest Goebbels. The major, leading a detachment of helmeted soldiers, rushed into Goebbels' office, pointing a pistol. He told the propaganda chief that he was under arrest. Goebbels, thinking fast, calmly reminded the major that he had sworn an oath to obey Hitler.

"Hitler is dead!" the major snapped.

"Impossible! I have just spoken to him. I will prove it."

Goebbels snatched up a phone and ordered the operator to connect him to Hitler at Wolf's Lair.

Goebbels was bluffing. He had heard that there had been an explosion at Wolf's Lair, but communication from Hitler's headquarters to Berlin had been garbled by the blast. Now he was gambling that Hitler had survived.

Incredibly, he had. Hitler had walked out of the flaming building, his face black, his hair singed, his uniform shredded. Four men were carried out dead or dying, and almost everyone else in the room had been injured. But Hitler had been saved by that block of wood between himself and the bomb.

At Wolf's Lair he was told that Goebbels wished to speak to him. Goebbels heard Hitler's hollow voice shouting, "Yes?"

Smiling, Goebbels handed the phone to the major. The major identified himself. Hitler ordered him to arrest the conspirators. "Yes, my Fuehrer!" the major shouted.

Within a few hours Stauffenberg and the plotting generals had been captured. That night Stauffenberg stood proudly in front of a wall, the rifles of a firing squad aimed at his gray tunic, stripped of his medals. He shouted, "Long live our sacred Germany!" and then was torn apart by a half dozen bullets. Other generals were handed revolvers and told to shoot themselves.

At Wolf's Lair, Hitler told Mussolini, who had arrived after the explosion for a visit, "Nothing is fated to happen to me, all the more so since this isn't the first time I have miraculously escaped death."

Moments later, glaring at those around him, Hitler vowed revenge on all the plotters. "I'll put their wives and children into concentration camps," he shouted, "and show them no mercy."

Even Stauffenberg's eighty-five-year-old grandfather, along with his daughters and sons, was imprisoned. Thousands of men, women, and children were arrested and tortured into admitting that they knew of the conspiracy. Hitler suspected that even his Desert Fox, General Rommel, had plotted to kill him, although he hadn't. He told Rommel to commit suicide or watch his family be murdered. Rommel swallowed poison and died almost instantly.

"The plotters," growled Hitler, "must be hanged like cattle." Nooses of piano wire were tied around their necks, the wire connected to meat hooks. The generals were forced to stand on tables, dressed only in pajama bottoms. The tables were kicked away, and the generals slowly strangled to death—while motion-picture cameras, at Hitler's order, filmed their death agonies. Hitler watched the movies, laughing, in his private theater at the Chancellery. His henchmen stared at the screen, pale-faced. Goebbels had to rush from the room, retching. The movie was Hitler's grim warning to all those around him: Follow me to the end or die like this.

More than 5,000 men and women—most of them innocent—were executed. Never again would there be a plot to kill Hitler. His frightened generals, his battered and bandaged soldiers, and his terror-stricken German people would now follow this demented, hysterical warlord, pulling his sputtering war machine down the last few miles of a road that ended at an abyss.

19
"Collapse and Panic Among the Americans!"

In a long gray line the uniformed German generals strode into the squat concrete bunker at Hitler's western front headquarters outside a small village in France. Inside, they saw two rows of black-uniformed SS men, armed with rifles, forming a lane that was lined on each side with chairs. At the head of the chairs, sitting in what looked almost like a throne, was Hitler. He was bunched up in the chair. His body shook uncontrollably. His face was pale and puffed, his blue eyes watery, his mouth half-open. His left arm twitched violently even as he gripped it with his right.

Hitler stood as the generals sat down in the chairs, the SS men standing above them. These were Hitler's personal 200-man body-guard. Ever since the bomb that had failed to kill him in July, 1944, Hitler was ringed by bodyguards. "None of us," said a general later who had attended this meeting in Hitler's head-quarters, "would have as much as dared to pull out a handker-chief."

The time was late November, 1944. Hitler had summoned his

generals to his headquarters to tell them of his latest plan to stop General Eisenhower's armies from overrunning Germany.

His back bent, dragging one foot behind him, Hitler walked to a wall map, now—at only fifty-five—a man who looked nearly seventy. With a pointer Hitler located the Ardennes Forest, that hilly and wooded area in Belgium where he had sprung his tanks to win the Six Weeks' War four years earlier. Again, he told his generals, he would gather all his strength and hide it in the Ardennes. It would be an army of 250,000 of his best fighters, spearheaded by all the tanks and armored cars he could muster, and covered by German fighter planes. They would rocket out of the Ardennes and smash into Eisenhower's American infantrymen, punching a huge hole through the Allied lines. The Americans would panic and run, he told his generals; he had seen it happen a hundred times during World War I. The American, a breed of people mixed in a melting pot, did not have the courage to fight. And the defeat would set off angry words between the British and the Americans, breaking up their alliance. Then they would be willing to talk peace with Germany.

The idea for the Ardennes offensive had come to Hitler a few weeks earlier. By now he had become convinced that the Allies knew his every move. (They did, because of the code breakers.) Hitler thought the Allies had a spy hidden in the Chancellery. At a meeting in the Chancellery he had ordered his troops to fall back to Germany for a "last-ditch defense." Then he had called a few of his generals into an inner room, where no one could spy on them, where he told them, "I have made a momentous decision. I am taking the offense. Here—out of the Ardennes!" And he had slapped his fist onto a map.

Later he told a trusted aide that if the Ardennes offense did not succeed, "I no longer see any possibility for ending the war well. But we will come through! A single breakthrough on the western front! You'll see! It will lead to collapse and panic among the Americans. We'll drive right through their middle and take Antwerp . . . a tremendous pocket will encircle the entire English army, with hundreds of thousands of prisoners. . . ."

Later the aide, looking at the sinking production rate of the smoking German factories, said, "Hitler is playing his last card—and knows it, too." And he added, "Our factories will have stopped turning out guns and ammunition by January 1, 1946."

To play his last card, Hitler had to take a risk that made his generals frown. Planes, tanks, and troops had to be stripped from the eastern front, where they had been battling the Russians. His generals had warned him: "The eastern front is like a house of cards. If the front is broken through at any one point, all the rest will collapse." They warned that the Russians were building up strength for an offense. Hitler scoffed at the warnings and ordered the troops and supplies sent to the west for the Ardennes offensive.

Hitler, still convinced that a spy lurked in his Chancellery, kept the plans for the Ardennes close to his chest. As a result, the code breakers—though they picked up Hitler's orders to create a new panzer army—did not learn of the coming offense, which the Germans called Operation Autumn Mist.

On the morning of December 16, 1944, through a swirling fog, the mighty German army—led by roaring tanks—crashed over the surprised Americans, and once more Hitler's panzers snarled toward the Channel ports, another gray dagger lunging to cut the Allies in half. Within a few days the Germans had pushed a huge bulge in the middle of the American line—and to Americans this battle would forever be known as the Battle of the Bulge.

But the small city of Bastogne sat, like a boulder, in the path way of the German thrust. Both the Americans and Germans raced to occupy the city. The American 101st Airborne Division—15,000 tough paratroopers—won the race. Their trucks screeched down Bastogne's cobblestoned streets only a few hours before German tanks poked their guns over a ridge on the other side of town.

The German armored cars and tanks formed a ring around the town as snow and icy winds whipped into the faces of the Americans, who were cut off from food and ammunition. German tanks and artillery poured a withering fire into the town. Then the Germans sent a messenger to the Americans, demanding their surrender. If they didn't surrender, the Germans warned, they would be annihilated by the heavy German guns. The 101st's commander, General Anthony McAuliffe, replied to the demand with one word—a word that made Americans proud and threw into Hitler's teeth his charge that Americans panicked and ran. Replied McAuliffe: "Nuts!"

Day after day the Germans rained shells into Bastogne. But when they charged, they were met by streams of fire from the hungry, cold, exhausted Americans. On Christmas Day the GI's ate the last of their cold C rations. But the next day American tanks broke through the German lines to bring food and ammunition to the cheering paratroopers.

A furious Hitler ordered heavier attacks on Bastogne. Without that city the Germans could not push a deeper bulge into the American middle. But despite wave after wave of German assaults, the Americans held on, while the snow-covered fields around the city became spattered with blackened wrecks of tanks and the corpses of gray-coated Germans.

For a week the battle raged. Then the reinforced Allied armies began to bite into the bulge from each side. The Germans, seeing they could be cut off, had to retreat. For Eisenhower the victory had been a bloody one: More than 8,000 Americans were dead, another 48,000 wounded. But more than 100,000 Germans—the cream of Hitler's army—had been killed, wounded, or captured in the furious assault. And as the Germans wearily slogged back toward the German border, they left behind the iron muscle of their panzer army, more than 600 tanks and 6,000 trucks now crumpled, burned-out wrecks on snow crimsoned by the blood of both sides.

Hitler had learned that Americans did not run. And he had made his final lunge for victory.

In the east, a few days later, that house of cards collapsed. A charging Russian army smashed through the weakened German lines in Poland, then streaked across the flat plains of central Europe like an express train, headed on a direct line for Berlin.

Germany was now caught between two giant pincers—Eisenhower's armies charging from the west, and the Russians from the east. Meanwhile, Allied air armadas carpeted Germany with bombs that turned cities, said one horrified spectator, "into forests of flames."

In his Berlin Chancellery Hitler ordered boys of fifteen and men of sixty to put on uniforms. "I expect you to defend Germany's sacred soil," he told them by radio. "None of us gives up a square foot of German soil while he is still alive!"

Then, like an animal being chased, Hitler went underground. He descended from his Chancellery to a concrete bunker under the building as Allied bombers rocked Berlin. The bunker, with a twelve-foot-thick roof of concrete, could withstand even a direct hit on the Chancellery above it. And the bunker was large enough to house Hitler's staff of several hundred—bodyguards, secretaries, servants, and cooks and General Staff. In this tomb Hitler lived like a madman through the last weeks of his life.

A general who visited him was shocked by his appearance:

> Physically, he presented a dreadful sight. He dragged himself about painfully and clumsily, throwing his torso forward and dragging his legs after him from his living room to the

conference room of the bunker. He had lost his sense of balance; if he were detained on his brief journey (75 to a hundred feet), he had to sit down on one of the benches that had been placed along either wall for this purpose, or else cling to the person he was talking to. . . . His eyes were bloodshot; although all documents intended for him were typed out in letters three times ordinary size, on special "Fuehrer typewriters," he could read them only with strong glasses. Saliva frequently dripped from the corners of his mouth.

Hitler, Allied doctors later learned, had been stricken with at least one heart attack. In addition, he may have been suffering from Parkinson's disease, which results in a shaking of the body and trembling of the limbs. But he had also been weakened by his own doctors, who gave him drugs containing strychnine, a weakening and even fatal poison, to calm his nerves and ease the pain of severe stomachaches during the last two years of the war.

But the German people still imagined Hitler as strong and dominant, even as Russian and Allied armies drove across a burning Germany toward Berlin. Any German room in which his picture hung, a few Germans still believed, would not be flattened by a bomb—even though hundreds of thousands of such rooms had already been leveled. In an almost childlike faith in Hitler as a miracle worker, both German civilians and top generals believed he had developed, waiting to spring on the unsuspecting enemy, "a secret weapon" that would change defeat into victory. Some thought the secret weapon was a "death ray" to kill advancing troops. Others thought it was a rocket-propelled bomber, like the small V-2 "buzz bombs" that had been shot at English cities. And a few hinted that the secret weapon might even be a product of research that German scientists had been conducting for years—splitting the atom.

(But Americans had also won that race, and soon, on a New

Mexico desert, they would explode the first atomic bomb, the climax of research begun at the suggestion of the great scientist Albert Einstein, a Jew Hitler had driven from Germany. Later, in 1945, the Americans would drop A-bombs on the Japanese cities of Hiroshima and Nagasaki, causing Japan to surrender and finally bringing an end to World War II.)

"Things are bad," Germans told one another, huddled in air-raid shelters as B-17's thundered overhead by the thousands, "but things have been bad before and Uncle Adolf saved us. He will save us again."

But Uncle Adolf was no longer the blustering fiery-eyed warlord. He slept for a few hours each afternoon in his bedroom in the bunker, then tried to work through the night. His conferences with his General Staff usually ended at six in the morning. Then his secretaries arrived, and Hitler gave them orders for the day.

"With shaking legs and quivering hand," one said later, "he stood facing us for a while and then dropped exhausted down on the sofa again. His servant would prop up his feet. He lay there completely torpid, filled with only one thought . . . chocolate cake. Whereas in the past he had eaten at most three pieces of cake, he now had the platter handed to him three times, and heaped his own plate each time . . . he virtually did not talk at all."

When he did talk, he blamed others for the fiery disaster above him. "We have had unexpected setbacks because my orders were not followed," he told his generals in March, 1945, when the Russian armies were only 100 miles from Berlin. And he told someone else, "I want them to write on my tombstone: 'He was the victim of his generals.'" To a secretary he growled, "I can rely on no one. I am lied to on all sides. They all betray me."

Then, in the middle of April, he was suddenly lifted into a mood of exultation. America's President, "that Jew-loving Roosevelt, he's dead!" he shrieked, waving a newspaper clipping. President Roosevelt had died suddenly. "Here we have the miracle I always predicted," he said, his voice again reverberating. "The war isn't lost. Read it! Roosevelt is dead!"

Now, Hitler thought in his fantasies, the Americans would pull back their armies and join him in fighting Russian communism. A few days later, he had a new fantasy. He told Goebbels and his wife, who now lived in the bunker with their six children, that "the Russians are going to suffer their bloodiest defeat" when they attack Berlin.

He was cut off from reality. He sat for hours in front of drawings. They were professional renderings of the drawings he had done as a teenager in Linz, drawings of bridges and buildings of a new Linz. "Look," he told General Keitel one day, "see what I plan to do in Linz. There will be the finest works of architecture in the world. . . ." Keitel stared. A few days earlier American troops had linked up with the Russians in the city of Linz.

For hours he stood in front of a wooden model of the future city of Linz. That had been the dream of his youth, to be a famous artist and architect, and perhaps now Hitler wanted to escape back to that youth and those dreams.

One morning he snatched up a phone and called the general commanding the troops defending Berlin. He ordered an immediate attack on the advancing Russians.

Keitel, anxiously rubbing his hands, tried to dissuade Hitler. "There are not enough troops, my Fuehrer," protested Keitel.

"Yes, there are," Hitler snapped, slamming down the phone. And he rattled off the names of seven divisions.

Keitel's jaw dropped. Those seven divisions had been wiped out a year earlier in Russia.

Eva Braun had flown to the besieged Berlin. Her arrival in the underground bunker was like a chilling breeze down the spines of the people in the bunker, for they knew what her coming meant: She wanted to die with Hitler. Gently, Hitler tried to persuade her to fly south to the Bavarian mountains, where Goering and other Nazi leaders had already fled. But "the loneliest woman in Germany" had decided that her days of loneliness were over. She stayed.

As Berlin burned above them and Russian troops gunned down thirteen-year-old German soldiers only a few blocks away, Hitler and Eva Braun were married just before midnight on April 28, a few days after his fifty-sixth birthday. After sipping a glass of champagne, Hitler took Eva's arm and said, "We will retire now. I wish to be awakened only when a Russian tank stands outside." He glanced around the room at the wedding guests: his two women secretaries, the blunt-faced Martin Bormann, the wizened Goebbels and his blond wife, Hannah, their six children, and a few generals and other officers.

"But what does all that matter?" Hitler said, escorting his new wife out of the room with trembling arms. "Sooner or later everyone has to leave all such nonsense behind."

For the past few days Hitler had been urging one of his generals to battle with his army into Berlin, throw out the Russians, then hold the city. But by the evening of the next day, April 29, Hitler told Goebbels and the others in the bunker that the army would not arrive to rescue them. By now Hitler had learned that Himmler and Goering—in other parts of Germany—had asked the Allies for a cease-fire. He called both traitors and ordered SS men to shoot them down.

Both escaped and were later captured by the Russians or Americans. Word also came that Mussolini had been captured and killed by Italian rebels, his body strung up by its feet in a gas station.

"I will not fall into the hands of the enemy dead or alive!" Hitler said softly. "After I die, my body shall be burned and so remain undiscovered forever."

His generals urged him to try to fly from Berlin to the south. But he replied quietly that he would stay in Berlin. To Albert Speer, who had headed German industry, he said, "I have resolved to stay here. . . . I shall not fight personally. There is always the danger that I would only be wounded and fall into the hands of the Russians alive. I don't want my enemies to disgrace my body either. I've given orders that I be cremated. [My wife] wants to depart this life with me and I'll shoot Blondi beforehand. Believe me, Speer, it is easy for me to end my life. A brief moment and I'm free of everything, liberated from this painful existence."

It would be better, he told Speer, if Germany and its people also were destroyed. "For the nation has proved to be the weaker, and the future belongs solely to the stronger eastern nation. In any case, only the inferior will remain after this struggle, for the good already have been killed."

But even in these final moments he could not forget what had been the number one enemy in his imagination since he had shuffled through the Vienna underworld as a tramp: the Jews. He had not been hard enough in stamping out the Jews, he told his secretaries. "Now," he said, "they have sent their armies to destroy me." He shrugged. "Life," he said, "forgives no weaknesses."

On the morning of April 30 Hitler awoke to be told that a unit of Russians now held the street adjacent to the bunker. Russian shells were falling into the courtyard outside the bunker. No one could stick a head outside the bunker and survive in that storm of flying metal. Hitler's exhausted troops cowered behind buildings, sleepless for days, short of ammunition, knowing more bloody fighting was useless, yet mechanically pulling triggers like robots, obedient to the end to Hitler's final orders to die before surrendering.

Hitler lunched with his cook and several of his secretaries, chatting as though this April 30 were like any ordinary day. But after lunch he summoned Goebbels and Bormann and told them he was going to commit suicide. He had several small vials of cyanide and he handed one to each of his secretaries. Earlier, to make sure that the poison was strong enough, he had ordered an SS man to force a vial of it down the throat of Blondi. The dog had died almost instantly. A few minutes later Hitler passed by. He glanced with seeming indifference at the corpse of what Goebbels had once called "his closest friend."

He and Eva shook hands with Goebbels, Bormann, and the weeping secretaries. There were tears glistening in Hitler's eyes, and his face was a waxy yellow. He was dressed in a brown uniform with black boots. Eva wore a black dress. They walked into their apartment and closed the door behind them.

Hitler and Eva sat on a couch. She swallowed the vial of poison and flopped sideways on the couch at Hitler's side. At approximately three thirty on the afternoon of April 30, 1945, Hitler picked up his pistol, the same pistol that he had fired into the ceiling of the beer hall at the start of his putsch. Perhaps he glanced at a photo of his mother on a nearby table.

He pointed the pistol at his right temple. He pulled the trigger. The shot echoed down the concrete corridors of the bunker.

About the same time, in what one historian has called "a preposterous climax" to a life filled with bizarre happenings, some of Hitler's cooks and servants began to dance to loud music, unaware that the Fuehrer had just killed himself. They were dancing, singing, and drinking champagne to ease the strains of imminent death. (Some were killed by the Russians during the next few days when they fled the bunker.) So music, shouts, and happy laughter were the background sounds as Hitler died. Even though the men and women were told to quiet down, they continued to laugh and sing as Hitler's corpse was carried upstairs and out of the bunker. To millions of people, however, the sounds would not have seemed preposterous. What could have been more fitting than revelry for a world suddenly released of Hitler?

Bormann and Goebbels heard the shot and dashed into the room. They saw Eva's head flopped over on the arm of the sofa and Hitler's blood-smeared face resting on a low table.

The bodies were carried upstairs to the courtyard and doused with gasoline. Shuttling back and forth as shells exploded around them, SS men set fire to the corpses. They saw flames leap high and smelled the acrid odor of burning flesh. Goebbels, Bormann, and the SS men flashed the Nazi salute—the last for Adolf Hitler.

A week later Germany surrendered. Hitler's Third Reich had fallen. Most of his accomplices were tried for the murders they had committed. But Goebbels escaped the hangman's noose by poisoning himself, his wife, and their children in the bunker two days after Hitler's suicide. Himmler, after his capture, also died by poison. Goering, too, swallowed poison after being convicted of war crimes. Other top Nazis were hanged or sentenced to jail terms for as long as life. Rudolf Hess, who had flown to Britain during the war on "a peace mission," was still sitting in a bare cell in a prison near Berlin some thirty-two years after the war's end. But no trace was ever found of Martin Bormann, the man who secretly ruled Germany. Some thought he had been killed in the last days of the war; others claimed he was still alive, hiding out in a remote South American village.

For years there were rumors that Hitler was still alive. He had fled Berlin, the stories went, and was hiding in South America.

But the Russians found his charred remains buried in a shell hole in the bunker courtyard. From dental records Russian doctors proved that these were the ashes of the man who had come so close to conquering half the world.

Hitler's success may have been the weight that brought him down, a hunted animal, to that ignoble grave. Inflated by the cheers of millions and intoxicated by his blinding successes, Hitler thought he could do no wrong—that he could lie, cheat, even murder nations as well as people.

He thought he had become a god. What he had become was first a gangster chief, then a tyrant, then a mass murderer, and—certainly at the end—a madman.

Perhaps no one summed up Adolf Hitler better than his boyhood chum Gustl Kubizek. Years after Hitler died, Gustl had become a musical conductor in Vienna, that city where he and Hitler sought "to become somebody." In talking about the dead Hitler, Gustl once said, "What were God's intentions when he created this man?"

There can be no answer to that question. But we might pray that God will never create another one like him.

Index

Adolf Hitler (Toland), 181

Beck, Gen. Ludwig, 144–45, 146
Benes, Eduard, 147–48, 151–52
Bismarck, Otto von, 27, 96, 127
Blomberg, Gen. Werner von, 132, 135–36
Bormann, Martin, 80, 144, 179, 182, 211, 213, 214
Brauchitsch, Field Marshall Walther von, 144–45, 166, 180
Braun, Eva, 178–79, 198, 210–11, 213, 214
Bulge, Battle of the, 205–7

Chamberlain, Neville, 139, 147, 148–49, 151, 152, 153, 166
Chaplin, Charlie, 56
Churchill, Sir Winston, 152, 166, 169, 174, 179, 182, 199
Communist Party, 88, 89, 90, 91–95

Daladier, Édouard, 147, 148–49, 151, 166
Drexler, Anton, 49, 50, 51–52, 53
Dunkirk evacuation, 169–70

Einstein, Albert, 209
Eisenhower, Gen. Dwight D., 197, 204, 206
Enabling Act, 95–96

Ferdinand, Archduke Franz, 44
Franck, Hans, 86
François-Poincet, André, 125
Fritsch, Gen. Werner von, 132, 135–36

German Workers Party, 49, 50–52. *See also* National Socialist German Workers Party
Gestapo, 89, 94, 105, 113, 145
Godin, Lt. Michael von, 71
Goebbels, Hannah, 211

219

The Author

John Devaney, a free-lance writer, is the author of numerous books and articles. He lives in New York with his wife, Barbara, and two sons, John, Jr., and Luke.